# The Taste Makers:
## How New World Foods Came to Old World Kitchens

By
# Vicki Oppenheimer

Illustrated by
*Mona Luisa Diogo*

A Joint Publication of
Milpah Press and FLF Press. All rights reserved.

First Edition Published in the U.S. in December, 2003

Library of Congress Card Catalogue No. Pending
ISBN No. 0-9722707-1-X

# Table of Contents

# Preface –
# Who Were "The Taste Makers"?

The name "Taste Makers" didn't come to me in a flash. My mother was a good cook, and so I thought all food tasted good. Later in high school and college I began to eat in cafeterias and discovered that not all food tastes delicious. When I became a homemaker I bought cookbooks to master French and Italian cuisine, to explore such dishes as Asian satays, and to learn about our own distinctive southern recipes. Along the way I discovered that every ingredient can play many roles. A potato can be peasant fare, or it can be haute cuisine.

Ninety percent of the food we eat comes from plants, directly from the soil or from the herbivores that eat grasses and grains. Before a plant becomes a savory dish it needs to be identified as edible, not toxic, and it needs to be domesticated, sown, harvested and perhaps modified. All this must take place before a recipe can be written and a dinner served.

Who started such an elaborate undertaking and brought us such variety in food? To find the answer we must go back about 12,000 years to the nomadic hunters who followed herds of huge beasts across a land bridge from Siberia to the Americas. At the outset the hunters found unwary prey and hunting was easy and adequate for their needs. The women on the other hand must have been dismayed to discover that the plants in the New World were different from any they had encountered in the old country, and they had to learn which ones were good to eat and how to prepare them.

As populations grew and prey became scarce, the nomads were forced to settle down and plant seeds to provide food. These early agriculturists survived, but it took thousands of years for them to learn how to cultivate corn, potatoes, tomatoes and other nutritious foods. Generation after generation expanded the American menu, and in 1492 when Columbus arrived on a Caribbean island he found a robust people who could entertain him with a hearty feast.

It was the chili pepper that persuaded Columbus that he had found India. Later voyagers knew better. The European explorers who sought gold and silver brought cattle and wheat to the New World. They returned to their homelands laden with corn, tomatoes, potatoes, chilies and other foods which eventually proved to be more precious than gold. This transfer, sometimes called the Columbian exchange, revolutionized the way people eat in Europe and the Americas. The world's food resources were enormously increased; peasants had more to eat, aristocrats dazzled their guests with new dishes! Each country adapted the new food to suit its taste, its resources and its culture.

New World foods now constitute 62% of the world's total food consumption, and the New World pioneers who domesticated and cultivated unknown plants that have traveled around the world deserve to be called "The Taste Makers."

# 1
## History on Recipe Cards

In my files are 80 year-old recipe cards. I have cherished them because they are crammed with memories - they are not just recipes, they are history. The boxes are now in a storage closet, dog-eared, limp and yellow. The recipes are out-of-date but I haven't the heart to throw them away. Occasionally I take them out and linger over them, telling myself that I want to study an original recipe, but actually I want to hear my mother's voice and recall her feverish preparations for memorable feasts. I remember papa's favorite foods and his stories of a Russian childhood in the small village, the shtetl, where he grew up. The recipe for "babke", the yeast bread mother baked on wintry mornings, brings back the heady aroma of the past, and with it comes a story, not only of the bread but the great changes in our lives when my immigrant family became home owners. As I write these words the smell of babke seems to be floating through the air, so I can't resist telling you the story of how it happened that Mama made babke for breakfast on wintry mornings starting in 1919.

On a bright Saturday morning in May, 1919, Mama suggested that we take a walk. Papa, still at the breakfast table was surprised. "So where are we going?" Mama was already putting on her jacket, "Come, I'll show you."

I tagged along and tried to keep pace as Mama walked briskly for about half a mile to the outskirts of our Bronx neighborhood. She stopped in front of a squat, red brick house perched at the top of a long flight of steps. Mama looked at us questioningly, "You want to see inside the house?"

Papa laughed, "You're going to buy a house?" Mama, lowering her voice confided, "The bank is in a hurry to settle an estate, and is selling the house at a big sacrifice. This opportunity we shouldn't pass up. I got the keys from the bank so just let's have a look."

Papa looked skeptical. "This is a very inconvenient location, no trolley, no subway. It's very far from the kid's school." I was the "kid" in the fifth grade of P.S. 44. Mama looked at me and could see that I was delirious with excitement. Mama spoke carefully, as though she was thinking aloud, "The kid might have a little room with her own desk."

I nodded sagely, "This looks like a very nice house and it's not too far from school."

Papa offered other objections but Mama had a ready reply, "If the house was perfect we couldn't afford it."

By mid-July we were living in Mama's dream house. She painted the kitchen walls, sewed niñon curtains, crocheted antimacassars for the new sofa and hung the huge, old-fashioned family portraits. Papa pruned the privet hedge, installed a shower in the basement and whitewashed the basement walls. On balmy evenings my brother, sisters and their friends, gathered on the stoop of the house to play charades, twenty questions, and other games that young grown-ups play. Mosquitoes were chased with fly-swatters; a few were discouraged by the citronella candles.

October arrived with nasty cold winds. Instruction book in hand, Papa took to the basement and tried to unravel the intricacies of the coal furnace. His routine started at five in the morning: opening the damper, shaking down the ashes, shoveling coal and waiting impatiently for a sign of heat. A chorus of knocks, rattles and bangs meant that the radiators were preparing to let off a little steam, but not immediately.

In the kitchen, Mama lit the gas stove to dispel the damp cold. It was not her nature to waste a hot oven so she designed a plan. Every evening before she went to bed she prepared a batter for Babke, a sweetened Polish/Russian yeast bread. It rose slowly in the icebox and in the morning was ready for the oven. The aroma of a yeast bread in the oven routed us out of bed and filled our hearts with joy. Here is the recipe.

# *Babke*

1 cake of yeast

1 cup warm milk

$^1/_4$ teaspoon salt

¾ cup sugar

$3^3/_4$ cups flour

$^1/_2$ cup unsalted butter

3 eggs, beaten

$^1/_2$ cup raisins

1 tablespoon grated lemon rind

Soften the yeast in a small amount of the warm milk, when it begins to bubble add the remainder of milk, salt, a teaspoon sugar and one cup of flour. Beat well and set aside to rise.

In a large bowl cream the butter with the remaining sugar. Add the beaten eggs and the bubbling yeast mixture. Beat thoroughly. Add the raisins and the lemon rind and the remainder of the flour. Mix until the batter is thick and smooth. Cover and let rise in a warm place until batter is doubled in bulk.

Divide the batter in half and place each half in a well-greased 8 inch cake pan. Put the pans into the icebox. In the morning put the pans in a 375-degree preheated oven. Mama judged oven temperature by putting her hand inside the oven and counted how long she could keep her hand there. Brushed with melted butter and sprinkled with a little sugar and cinnamon, the bread baked for 45 minutes.

\* \* \*

Turn the clock back ten thousand years and find hunter-gatherers in the mountains of the Fertile Crescent, in southeast Turkey or Iraq. They make a gruel of pounded wild grain and water and leave it to dry on a hot stone in the sun. Behold, the gruel has turned into a flat bread. That revelation triggered an explosion of human ingenuity. Wild seeds were sown, harvests were reaped, wheat was milled and turned into flour. The hunter-gatherers became farmers. Tortillas, matzos, chapatis and other unleavened breads had their beginning in that era of innovation.

But leavened bread, like babke, probably came later, as a happy accident that occurred in Egypt. When a wheat batter became contaminated by airborne yeast, the yeast created the carbon dioxide needed to make a raised loaf. The Egyptians continued to use a piece of raised batter to knead into new bread batches — a sourdough method still popular, especially in San Francisco. The Hebrews and Romans learned the technique and copied it. In Exodus 012.015 the Israelites received the command "Seven days shall ye eat unleavened bread....ye shall put away leaven out of your houses." Observant Jews still celebrate the Passover holiday by eating matzos for seven days and reciting the story of the Exodus at the Passover feast, the Seder.

When Louis Pasteur, in mid-nineteenth century identified yeast as a living organism, raised bread was viewed with distrust by so-called health authorities. Ultimately yeast led to vastly improved culturing techniques and contemporary opinion finds yeast a healthful food, a good source of vitamins.

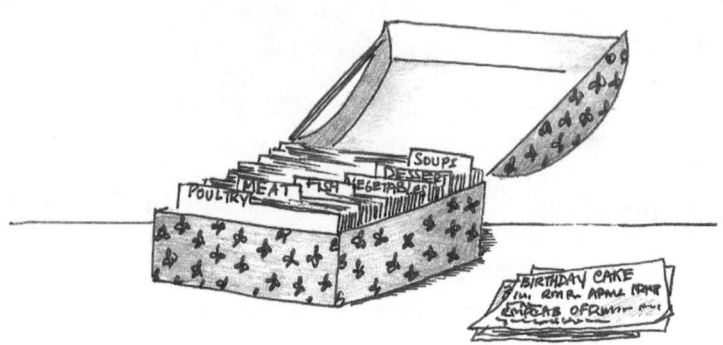

I see my recipes as a record of tumultuous events. I was just a child at the onset of the First World War, but I vividly remember selling Liberty bonds "to beat the Kaiser." The newspapers reported that about one-third of the men called for the draft were found to be so poorly nourished that they had to be rejected for army service. The war forced us to begin thinking seriously about healthful eating.

In 1912 people learned that rickets, pellagra and beriberi were vitamin deficiency diseases. Vitamins became household words and new vitamin discoveries continued to make front-page news. In my childish handwriting a recipe card says

## "Don't pour vitamins down the drain, save vegetable cooking water because it contains vitamins."

During the war nutrition awareness became a government priority, but not until 1946, following World War II, did enrichment of white rice, flour and other foods that had been stripped of their original vitamin-rich bran layer become mandatory. Medical training did not include the study of nutrition, and new eating fads proliferated.

The 1930 economic depression was a melancholy time for people who had lost their jobs and were hard-pressed to put food on the table. Meat was costly. Bread, beans, rice, pasta and salads were more affordable and for a while many Americans were eating peasant foods—ironically we now know these foods to be nourishing and healthful. I remember the rent parties in New York's Harlem and Greenwich Village where each guest brought a covered dish, and would show off by bragging about its low cost. A small contribution helped the host pay the rent. Many of my artist friends living in cold-water flats and factory lofts during the depression later became well-known and respected painters and poets.

Monday morning, December 8, 1941, the day after Pearl Harbor, I waited on line to sign up for civilian defense duty along with thousands of other New Yorkers who had turned out to answer President Roosevelt's call for civilian volunteers. We overflowed onto the icy sidewalk outside the local public school. Stamping our feet and hugging our bodies, we railed against the Japanese who had attacked us at Pearl Harbor and we pledged our dedication to winning the war. While waiting for interviews we developed a buddy spirit and exchanged experiences.

An elderly gentleman who had served in the Merchant Marine during the First World War said New York City was a prime target for another sneak air attack. The greatest need was for street wardens, "spotters," who could comb the skies and watch for enemy planes.

As a busy wife, mother and freelance writer I had little time for volunteer work, but I was burning with win-the-war zeal. As an ardent bird watcher, accustomed to peering into the sky, I considered myself qualified for the street warden job, and I already had a good pair of binoculars. There was no time to lose and no consideration of the logistic problems that the Japanese would face in reaching our target city.

I didn't get the sky-watching job; to my dismay I had an interview with a lieutenant whose job was to recruit workers for the government agency dealing with wartime food shortages. Her little speech seemed rehearsed: "Young farmers will be going into the army, and there will be fewer hands to produce food for the war effort.

"We are facing serious shortages of meat, eggs, sugar, coffee, butter, and other farm products. We need innovative ideas for nutritious meals that make minimal demands on these limited resources. "With a flourish she ended her speech, "to win this war, rationing must be made to work".

I ended up serving as a volunteer in a government sponsored test kitchen, working with professional dieticians and home economists. I don't think we had any category called nutritionists, but we knew about the importance of vitamins and vitamin-rich plants. Our department developed a chicory-based coffee that was disdained as "ersatz", phony, but that filled a need. Other inventions that are still on grocery shelves include Spam, Tang (an orange drink that was eventually adopted for space flight) and oleomargarine (now familiar as Margarine).

New foods are likely to prove acceptable if they look and taste like familiar dishes. Achieving this during wartime was a great challenge, and much thought went into making new ingredients taste like familiar favorites.

Many years later, as a student of anthropology, I was struck by a remarkable parallel—the plants and animals of the New World were different from those of the Eurasian land mass. How did the pioneering migrants decide what plants were edible? How did they make them palatable? They needed to write a new menu that has now spread throughout the entire world.

# 2
# The Paleo-Indians

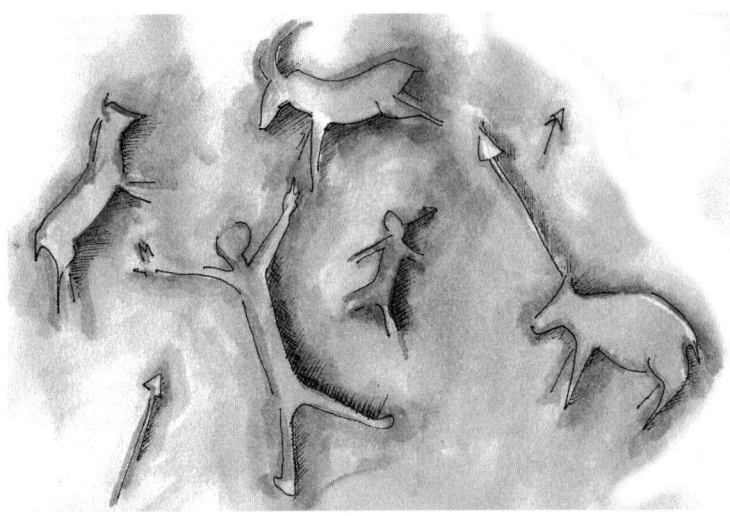

The "New World" was not new to the millions of people who had lived on the land for thousands of years before Columbus arrived. Where did these people come from? History does not reveal the full story, but radio-carbon dating and pollen-testing have given us some clues. Geologists and archeologists have also given us greater understanding of the past. The adventure story that emerges eclipses any of the myths created by Indian shamans and tops any script ever devised by Hollywood screen-writers.

The saga starts approximately 12,000 years ago, during the last glaciation of the Ice Age, when sea levels were about 325 feet lower than they are today. This left a thousand mile long land bridge from Siberia to the American continent that is today submerged. Nomadic hunters, following herds of huge beasts, crossed this bridge and arrived on the frozen tundra of the American continent.

These nomadic groups traveled with their hunting dogs. Their women, burdened with small children and household goods, trailed behind, foraging for wild plants. At the outset there was plenty of meat. The skilled hunters encountered unwary beasts. The women were bewildered to find that the plants of the new world were entirely different from the ones they had left behind. They experimented with unfamiliar greens, roasted strange roots, and eventually learned what plants seemed edible and which were dangerous.

When an ice-free corridor from the Yukon to Montana opened a pathway to a milder climate, the travelers entered a panoramic world with views of mountains and valleys, forests and streams, prairies and deserts. It was seemingly a land without end. There was room to move to the next valley, or to the high perch of a mountain peak. When game became scarce, small groups split away into new territories and eventually evolved into tribal societies. They stretched out across the American continents and in their travels they saw some familiar vegetation, including pine, oak and maple trees, but many of the trees and blossoms they saw were unknown to them and they must have wondered why there was such difference in plant life.

This continued to be a puzzle until development of the theory of continental drift by Alfred Wegener in 1912. The gymnosperms and angiosperms, namely pines, oak and maple trees, had already established themselves while all the continents were still connected in a single super-continent called *Pangea*. After *Pangea* split up into tectonic plates that evolved into the continents we know today (we can still see that the outlines of these continents fit together like pieces in a jig saw puzzle), these older varieties were found on all the continents, but any new species that evolved were found only on one of the separate continents. Furthermore, after the ice ages the ice that covered the continents receded at different rates and herbaceous flowering plants on the American continents developed at a different time from similar species elsewhere.

Plants are basically isolated and remain passive; they depend on birds, winds and people to spread their seeds. The wild plants that emerged from the icy tundra could not cross the sea, so they remained isolated and were strange to Europeans and Asians. It is the discovery of these plants that made possible the ecological exchange which has enriched the world's food supply and ultimately led to enormous increases in world population.

Plants also try to protect themselves from predators by developing toxins to ward off invasions of insects, fungi and animals. The newcomers to the American continents who were hunters had to augment their diets with plants, and they had to discover which plants were poisonous and which were safe. They collected greens and roots and learned how to make them more savory by heating, soaking or threshing. A diversity of plants provided a nutritious diet. People lived longer; more infants survived and were sturdier. Their population grew.

By 9000 B.C. many of the Ice-Age animals that had lured hunters to the New World became extinct. This massive die-off, known as the Pleistocene extinction, may have been caused by over-hunting. The tremendous number of weapons found in animal hides gives some credence to this supposition. Another hypothesis relates to drastic climate change. As the ice receded, heavily furred animals were perhaps unable to adapt to the warmer climate. Buffalo continued to graze on tall grass prairies long after more wooly animals had disappeared, but without horses, native people did not find buffalo easy prey.

The Pleistocene extinction profoundly changed the life of the people. Men had hunted cooperatively and were anchored by traditions to their ancestral hunting ground. When a man took a woman for his wife she was brought into his kinship society. Women gave up their own tribal identities and the children became integrated into the male society.

Sons learned the mystique of the hunt and were initiated into manhood within the father's kinship group.

When game became scarce, plants became the major source of food. The women shared their knowledge of grasses, tubers, roots, herbs, berries, fruits, nuts and seeds, and the entire community looked for plants to supplement meager portions of game. Plants sprouted thickly around refuse heaps, and that may have inspired the deliberate planting of seeds.

Seed planting meant settling down and tending crops. Home grounds that were familiar to women were the most productive. Young girls learned which plants could be dried, what flowers and grasses could be shredded into fiber for weaving. Children helped gather piñon nuts, sunflower seeds and acorns to store for the winters. They picked flowers and berries that made colorful dyes. They collected tree bark that alleviated pain, which contained the compound now known as aspirin. Some plants induced feelings of relaxation, others inspired gaiety. The women who gathered the plants knew their secrets and this secret knowledge helped them forge strong bonds of unity. Some tribes developed powerful matrilineal societies. Brides no longer needed to move to the hunting grounds of their husbands. Men moved to the tribal territory of their wives.

Men cleared the land, they dug ditches and terraces, and they were also the religious leaders. Agriculture called for great devotion and the men devised rituals that accompanied the sowing and harvesting for each season. They studied the phases of the moon, forecast the weather and knew the proper omens for each phase of growing crops. Both men and women studied the medicinal properties of plants and their knowledge became widespread. Populations grew rapidly. Those who were not involved in agriculture practiced other skills. Some devised new tools for hunting and plowing,

some studied the plants and learned their medicinal virtues, others indulged in the arts, painting fanciful figures. Artisans with great skill carved out monumental figures of stone to immortalize their gods. The wise men studied the heavens and envisioned the mysteries of religions that demanded prayer, devotion and sacrifice.

Populations spread into every region of the Americas. Small groups budded off from their communities and set out to form their own outposts. They traveled into new territories and adapted their beliefs to the new lands. Some migrants wandered as far as Tierra del Fuego at the tip of South America. In their wanderings they encountered new landscapes with unfamiliar plants, birds and animals and they developed new language to name their discoveries. By the time Columbus arrived on the scene, millions of people lived in the Americas. They spoke 2000 different languages, all with syntax and grammar. They had fanciful myths and they translated them into their own languages.

The precipitous decline in population after European contact makes it impossible to say how many native-Americans actually inhabited the continents. But it is estimated that the territory now covered by the United States may have been home to 15 million people.

Growing populations required more land. Forests were cut down, the trees were burned, and forested land was converted into acreage for planting. Slash and burn agriculture, where the ash from burned trees provides temporary fertilizer for farming, existed in all parts of the world, and wherever it was practiced it had devastating environmental effects.

Slash and burn, plus the encroachment onto new lands, led to tribal warfare that endured for centuries. Great empires emerged and built civilizations that have left their mark with awesome pyramids, terraces, stone work and woven fabrics. Millions of tourists come, look and marvel at the great works that sank into ruins over the centuries.

Their agricultural feats have also left an imprint on the land and we can still admire the milpah mounds of the Maya, the *chinampas*—floating islands—of the Aztecs, and the Andean terraces of the Inca. These hand-built terraces stretched for miles and supplied corn, potatoes, amaranth and quinoa for a huge population of people inured to the mountain air.

Botanical sleuthing has not revealed a clear picture of how early grasses, tubers and roots were turned into the foods we now savor. Artificial selection and cross-breeding have so altered the genetic make-up of plants that ancestral forms can no longer be identified. However, pollen profiles and radio-carbon dating tell us that cross-breeding and artificial selection practiced by the indigenous people proved amazingly successful. They adapted plants to a wide range of soils and climates.

These early Americans knew nothing of genes, but they seemed to have an intuitive understanding of how plants could be altered by cross-breeding. They had few materials with which to forge tools. The principle of the wheel was known to them but not applied to farming. There were no horses or oxen to pull a wheeled cart. Seeds, individually planted, were individually picked and examined for exceptional traits to be bred with a complementary variety. Their cross-breeding success seems almost mystical. They seemed to have uncanny prescience about the nourishment their plants provided.

Sixty percent of the entire world's diet now has its origin in New World plants. We enjoy corn, potatoes, tomatoes and sweet potatoes every day. What would we do without chocolate? What would Halloween be without a pumpkin? Peppers, mild and hot, add spice to life and are also good as painkillers.

History records the rise and fall of empires when fertile land was exhausted and turned into desert. There are hundreds of examples of species for which the discovery of a new food resource eventually resulted in extinction. The existing population feeds voraciously on the new food and the population increases exponentially. Then the food resource becomes inadequate for the larger population. Scarce food creates competition, fighting, destruction of habitat and ultimately extinction. Humans, using their wits, avert such disaster. Malthus and other doom-sayers have so far been proven wrong, and agricultural technology has increased production to the point where many countries now have to deal with surpluses. Despite this abundance we are plagued by worries over pesticides, fungicides, chemical preservatives and the loss of flavor in many foods. Some early agricultural methods have persisted among people who honor the traditions of their ancestors and we can still examine some of their methods.

## *Maya Soil Conservation*

Farmers of the Yucatan peninsula, heirs to Mayan tradition, do not use commercial fertilizers, herbicides or pesticides; they cannot afford to pay for such commercial farm aids. Like their ancient ancestors they believe in Nature's benevolence and plant according to ancient signals. There are no neat rows in their farm fields; these descendants of the Maya plant on milpahs, hilled mounds, which are scattered randomly. Each mound is built up on the previous year's planting and holds maize, beans and squash, the three foods that the Maya consider sacred. This felicitous combination has served them well. Eaten together, these vegetables complement each other and provide the amino acids and the complex proteins essential to human existence.

Milpah agriculture is very efficient. The corn stalk acts as a pole for the climbing beans; the beans reciprocate by providing nitrogen to the soil, and the broad prickly leaves and spiny vines of the squash keep the ground moist, discourage weeds, repel animal predation and prevent soil erosion.

American colonists adopted "hilling," similar to the milpah mound, and farmers followed this method until the 1930s, then it was abandoned in favor of dense planting and deep plowing. Deep plowing has resulted in the loss of thousands of tons of top soil each year. The Federal government is finally taking steps to halt this disastrous waste. The law now requires farmers to stem soil erosion and the popular method is by use of a conservation device called the no-till planter. It allows farmers to plant seeds in fields covered with the previous year's crops. This may enrich the soil rather than deplete it. Farmers who do not adopt this new method of no-till planting risk the loss of farm subsidies, but the method can hardly be called "new." It harks back to early Mayan milpahs.

The Mayans have become a highpoint of interest to American scholars. Decoding their literature, the Mayan Codex, opened the world's eyes to their brilliant achievements. They made significant advances in the fields of astronomy, writing, science, crafts, art and trade. Their calendar system is considered a mathematical marvel. But there is an unexplained hiatus. For 600 years from 300 A.D to approximately 900 A.D. they prospered; and then they mysteriously disappeared. Their zeal to create triumphant monuments in the Yucatan, Belize and Guatemala may have caused irreversible ecological disasters from which they were slow to recover. The ruins of the Mayan empire still inspire awe among tourists.

## *Aztec Wetland Agriculture*

The Aztecs invaded neighboring territories, enslaved prisoners and demanded tributes of food and metals, but their territorial expansion could not keep pace with their exploding population. Anthropologist Marvin Harris has proposed a theory that the Aztec religious rite of cannibalistic human sacrifice was a way of bringing more protein to a malnourished people. That theory is not universally accepted, but Harris makes a cogent argument for the Mexican need for greater food resources.

Mexico City rests on what was once a shallow lake. Around the perimeters of the lake the marshland was not suitable for draining or planting. But the Aztecs found a way of creating arable land by scooping up mud from the marshy borders of the lakes and holding it in place with mats of reeds, stones and brush. They created small artificial islands called *chinampas*, or "floating gardens" where they later planted trees whose roots anchored the islands to the earth. Water flowed through the ditches and more mud was added each year before planting to constantly increase agricultural production. *Chinampas* exist in the Mexican suburb of Xochimilco, and twenty years ago we rented canoes to take us to the islands. There we found women in colorful dress selling flowers and vegetables grown on the floating islands. They arranged the corn, squash, beans and peppers into flamboyant displays.

Now the floating gardens are known as the Ecological Park of Xochimilco. It is a popular tourist feature, just a one-hour boat trip from Mexico City. It is an educational outpost, a stopping-off place with a program stressing the protection of mangrove forests and wetlands. Mangroves, estuaries and wetlands are marvelously productive. They are seedbeds for fish and crustaceans, and an acre of mangrove forest can be far more productive than an acre planted in corn. Saving such areas becomes increasingly difficult when sunny tropical beaches beckon developers and tourists. Wetland legislation and mangrove protection clauses are now in force in many parts of the country, but shelter-belts in sensitive areas are often violated by short-sighted development.

## *Inca Biodiversity*

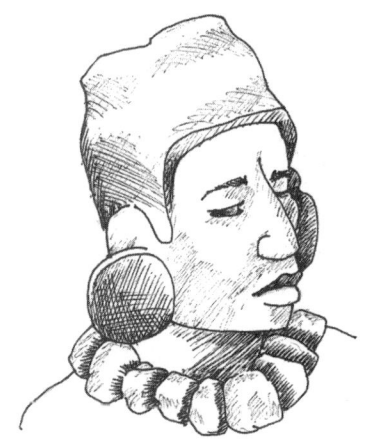

The steep slopes of the Andes are not hospitable to agriculture, and yet they actually proved to be a prime site for plant cultivation and experimentation. In 1532, at the time of the Spanish conquest, native people had been planting crops on the Andean mountain slopes for at least 3000 years. With digging sticks and bare hands they carved terraces to build ridged fields and irrigation ditches. From the heights of Machu Pichu or the hills around Lima the terraces dominate the landscape, but the terraces are now barren of crops.

The Inca, who dominated the lands now called Ecuador, Peru and Chile, were master builders and innovative farmers. Their terraces and farmlands reached to mountain heights where no trees could venture. The major crops were corn and potatoes. Corn grew at altitudes up to 8,000 feet. Potatoes survived at higher elevations and adapted to every environment. Quinoa, a plant that could tolerate the cold climate, grew at the very mountain top.

Potato plants became an Inca obsession. They were planted at every cusp of the mountain and were under constant observation. Careful note was taken of their growing progress. They were adapted to a wide range of soil and growing conditions. Cultivars were assessed for the hours of daylight needed for maturation, their tolerance for cold, and their adaptability to elevations of up to 15,000 feet. Some potatoes were sufficiently hardy to be stored for the winter, others thrived in milder climates. Thousands of potato varieties emerged in every shape, form and color. The entire enterprise was an experimental agricultural laboratory that yielded information that could be used to produce the best stock in the greatest quantities. The humble potato growers of the Andes who were once proud Quechuans still plant the seeds, inherited from their forebears, on their small plots of land.

In the Peruvian Andes stands a modern institution, the Centro Internacional de las Papas (CIP). It is a seed bank, a repository for computerized information on thousands of potato cultivars. This genetic material, a gift from the Inca, may some day be our insurance against disaster should an invasion of plant disease or blight threaten our current crops. There is also the danger that in our large-scale agriculture, where few varieties are planted, some pests may become resistant to the pesticides and fungicides on which we depend.

The seed bank is a world resource; it holds information gleaned from Inca terraces and modern agriculture, but seed banks are not totally reassuring. They may be vulnerable to violence, terrorism or electrical and economic failure. A vast accumulation of seeds in the Vavilov Library, in the former Soviet Union, was abandoned because of financial pressures on the government. Potato diversity still exists among the Quechuan and Aymara people, tucked away in small plots on the mountains, but this is a very tenuous resource.

In Ecuador and Peru, Andean farmers trudge down the slopes on market days carrying small sacks of potatoes, grown from seed inherited from generations of ancestors. Their potatoes come in many colors: blue, purple, yellow, red, white. They lay the potatoes out, one by one, between the women who are weaving hats and baskets and the lady who is selling love charms. We can hardly put our faith in the survival of such markets to provide us with assurance of biodiversity, but a stock of seed might reveal a cultivar resistant to an insidious pest, or one well suited to survive dry seasons.

At present agri-business concentrates on varieties best suited to economic interests. Bland potatoes suitable for chips and fries constitute 62% of the market. That limits the number of varieties grown, and by limiting choices we are robbing ourselves of the biodiversity that is in the best interest of our continued abundance. A monoculture is always in danger of being attacked by diseases still unknown to us. Besides, there are delicious potatoes that we could be enjoying if we had a greater choice.

Scenes from Otavalo Market in Ecuador, 1968.

# 3

# *The Europeans*

On the other side of the Atlantic, especially in the northern tier of Europe, periods of starvation were commonplace. Wheat did not always mature in the summer's short growing season. Rye, the predominant grain, was often assailed by plant disease. Frequent drought caused devastating famine. An emaciated, malnourished population was plagued by illness, but disease was commonly attributed to sin, divine retribution, curses and astronomical phenomena.

Peasants and workers on farms or in crowded cities knew only vile, unhygienic conditions. Personal and household cleanliness and sanitary food were practically unknown. Diseases of epidemic proportions sapped the energy of the dejected European continent.

But Europe was already poised for change. Church domination had held the continent in superstitious servitude for centuries, but the church was increasingly being challenged. As far back as 1233 Pope Gregory had established a papal inquisition to investigate heresy in France. On October 11, 1517, Martin Luther nailed to the church door at Wittenberg his ninety-five theses calling for a reformation of church practices. A secular establishment, ripe for an era of exploration, inventiveness and creativity, had a new world to conquer across the wide Atlantic.

The Mediterranean rim of Europe had grown rich trading with the Orient. The Ports of Venice and Turin had a shipping monopoly on spices, silks and perfumes which came to the continent at exorbitantly inflated prices. Middlemen along the route all took huge profits. Merchant princes became fabulously wealthy and vied with each other as patrons of the arts. The Renaissance was unfolding and musicians, scholars and scientists from Germany, Austria and Russia flocked to Florence and Siena while the rest of Europe struggled to recover from years of war and famine.

The discovery of the Americas changed the center of economic gravity. The Atlantic Ocean became the focus of maritime activity with Spain, Portugal, Britain, France, and Holland ready to grab their share of New World riches. The Portuguese 15th century design for a wooden caravel marked a great advance in shipbuilding. The caravel was a marvel of speed, maneuverability and seaworthiness. With its lateen sails, it could sail closer to the wind than any square-rigger. By hugging the west coast of Africa it could reach the Canaries and with favorable westerly trade winds sail across the ocean.

The frenzied activity of shipbuilding was hampered by shortages of wood. Forests had been denuded in much of Europe and deforestation had caused severe environmental damage. Paestum, a magnificent Grecian city and shrine, had become an uninhabitable malarial swamp when in Roman times tall, stately pines were cut for masts. The land, stripped of trees, became marshland. Only the buffalo with its tough hide could withstand the malarial mosquitoes. In 1943 when American soldiers landed in Italy during World War II, they found the ghost city of Paestum. The Medical Corps launched a pest-control campaign, killed off the mosquitoes, supplied personnel with quinine (an Andean Indian medicine), and Paestum's serene and stately temples emerged from hundreds of years of forgetfulness and neglect. Other areas of Europe suffered similar catastrophes because of reckless deforestation.

In its frantic search for timber, the British navy first turned to the Baltic region for trees, but when Atlantic sea routes were established, American oak forests supplied ship-builders in Spain, Portugal, Holland, as well as Britain. They all became major sea powers. This was an era of exploration that led to important advances in the sciences. Astronomy, magnetism and time-keeping were essential to successful navigation.

The Spanish disdain for the food of "savages" had an evolutionary base as well as an unreasoning bias. Human taste buds serve as signals, telling us what is safe to eat. As a fruit-eating species we love sweets and savor them. The craving for salt, common to all animals, also has a biological base. Acids that retard bacterial growth are sought by humans because they relieve blandness. Only bitter toxins offend our taste buds, they send warnings that the food may be poisonous and the natural reaction is to spit them out.

These characteristic taste sensations possess endless variations. Depending on geography and available food resources we learn what food is fit to eat. Likes and dislikes, established in childhood, stay with us throughout our lives. We set out to taste new foods as curiosities or as exotic experiences, and in times of famine people can be cajoled into trying unfamiliar food. We are most comfortable with foods we have known all our lives. With delicacies from every corner of the world now available to us, we have more sophisticated palates and are more venturesome in our diets; but in the time of Columbus, even the wealthy knew only beets, turnips, parsnips, cabbage, onions, leeks, cucumbers, peas, olives, mushrooms, asparagus and artichokes as vegetables. Wild herbs were occasionally used to add flavor to bland diets. Imported spices were luxuries, reserved for the wealthy. It took time for Europeans to learn to eat tomatoes, potatoes, squash, peppers and other American foods. It took much more time for American foods to gain acceptance. Once accepted, each American food found a distinct place in various different ethnic cuisines.

Without an understanding of nutrition, plant science and pharmacology were based on the "Doctrine of Signatures" which decreed that plants resembling human bodily parts were able to cure ailments associated with that part of the body. Hepatica was used as kidney medicine. Bloodroot was the cure for anemia. Mandrake, an herb whose split root resembled the lower limbs of a human figure, was endowed with supernatural sexual powers. Leeching, bleeding and other drastic and excruciating measures caused untold misery, but they all had scientific approval and were considered advances in medicine.

Foods were also endowed with miraculous properties; old wives' tales based on experiences with foods like garlic and onions often proved to be valid. Rumors that foods from the Americas were unsavory persisted, and plants from the Americas were too new to have accrued kitchen wisdom. In some cases it took extraordinary measures to make the new plants palatable to a suspicious population.

As early as 1577 a Spanish physician, Nicolas Monardes, said that the medicinal properties of the plants from America were more valuable than precious metals. This was not considered a scientific assessment, and although absolutely correct, it was not taken seriously. Eventually the vitamin-rich plants that Europe reluctantly accepted led to scientific research and technology, stimulated trade and industry, brought leisure, enjoyment and an explosion of artistic creativity.

Looking back we can see how New World foods became essential to cuisines throughout the world. They continue to be basic to a healthful diet. At the present time plant products constitute 90% of the food we eat, and of course animals are fed by plant-based food chains. We now look at the plants that prospered on the American continents and doff our caps to the pioneering agriculturists who became expert plant breeders.

# 4
# *Peppers, Sweet and Hot*

The cultivation of spice plants precedes the beginning of history. We know that for thousands of years spices were as precious as gold. Pepper from India was so valuable that in Greek and Roman times you could pay rent, fines or taxes by counting out the appropriate number of peppercorns. A handful of peppers was deemed a handsome royal gift. In England you actually used peppercorns as money for purchases.

Arabs controlled the spice trade and jealously concealed their sources. A tortuous land route linked caravans carrying spices to those Mediterranean cities which controlled the monopoly. The source of pepper, cinnamon and other spices was shrouded in mystery, Arabs encouraged outrageous tales of magical fountainheads from which the spices sprang, and these beliefs allowed middlemen to extract exorbitant prices and garner huge profits. City-states such as Florence, Turin and Venice amassed great wealth, while the rest of Europe endured hardships following years of war and famine.

The Renaissance could be nurtured in fortunate city-states. Merchant princes and noble families competed with each other and the Roman Church for the honor of becoming patrons of painting, sculpture and architecture.

To break the Mediterranean monopoly and share in the wealth from the spice-trade was the obsession of Columbus. His calculations led him to believe that the world was much smaller than it actually proved to be. New ship designs and advanced sailing techniques gave Columbus the courage to pursue his quest, unaware of how truly distant the oriental spice islands were. When he landed on a Caribbean island he was certain that he had navigated his vessels to the coast of India. It was an illusion that he treasured. The flora and fauna were different from anything he had envisioned in India, but he desperately wanted to believe he had reached his appointed destination and resolutely clung to that belief throughout his life.

He must have wondered "where are the gold-encrusted splendors Marco Polo described?" People were not dressed in fine robes, nor did they dwell in palaces. On the other hand, he recognized them as Easterners with dark skins, straight black hair, and

Oriental eye folds. A highly-seasoned morsel of food at a banquet hosted by a local chief convinced him that he was indeed in India and the fiery pod he ate was pepper.

In his Journal on January 15, 1493, he wrote "The land was found to produce much *aji*, the pepper of the inhabitants...they deem it very wholesome and eat nothing without it." (the word has its roots in Amerindian languages, as does the word *chili*). Columbus reasoned that if the hot food was pepper, the people were almost certainly Indians. Those names, woefully wrong on all counts, have been our legacy for more than 500 years.

Columbus clung to the belief that he had found India, despite the misgivings of other navigators, notably Amerigo Vespucci. Columbus had lost favor with Ferdinand and Isabella and the novelty of his voyages had faded. He was desperate to retrieve his reputation and organized another expedition, his fourth voyage across the Atlantic. He intended to sail west, past the islands he had discovered, until he arrived at lands recognized as Asia or Japan. This voyage was his last and it proved to be disastrous. He was marooned in Jamaica and forced to return to Spain. He died in 1506, a dispirited, unheralded navigator.

The Spanish Inquisition was formally established in 1475 and headed by the notorious Tomas de Torquemada. He became confessor to Ferdinand and Isabella in 1483 and they were under his spell. Torquemada did not actually seek to convert Jews, but wanted to seek out the "conversos" who had already converted to Christianity but who persisted in their old ways. He wanted to punish them and root out any semblance of "Judaizing," including Jewish foods and methods of food preparation. The era of torture and autos-da-fé had arrived, and in 1492 he ordered the expulsion of all those he labeled Jews. The expulsion of Jews from Spain and later from Portugal created an upheaval in Europe. Tens of thousands of Jews traveled to Turkey and Flanders, whence they migrated to France, Germany and eastward to Poland and Russia. They brought with them a knowledge of foods that were unknown in their new homes. The interchange of food tastes had begun, and it would soon be enormously increased by the introduction of foods from the Americas.

The Inquisition did not erase the specter of church heresy. Martin Luther had called for a reformation of church practices. A secular establishment, ripe for an era of exploration, inventiveness and creativity, had new worlds to conquer across the wide Atlantic and inside their own borders where immigrant populations brought new ideas, crafts and inspiration.

In 1502 Amerigo Vespucci discovered the northern shore of South America and explored about 6000 miles of coastline. He had evolved a system of computing exact longitude, replacing the old system of dead reckoning. It was a remarkable achievement. He arrived at a figure for the earth's equatorial circumference just 50 miles off the correct measurement. He announced that South America was a new continent, not part of Asia, and in 1507 the German cartographer Martin Waldseemuller put the name "America" on a map. The new continent summoned up fears of cannibals and grotesque monsters. European explorers described novel creatures such as the alligator, armadillo and the wild turkey, but the chili pepper was quickly accepted as pepper. It was mistakenly believed to be the precious spice of India and was in great demand throughout Europe. It added flavor to bland food, was a mild preservative, and it was also considered a mind stimulant and aphrodisiac.

True peppercorns are the dried berries of a climbing perennial shrub (piperine, *Piper nigram*). The berries are picked green and then dried. Black pepper is allowed to "ferment" in the sun in order to intensify its flavor. White pepper has the skin removed before drying and is milder and more suitable for gentler sauces. Green peppercorns are perishable, usually bottled in liquid, and added to soft cheeses, sauces and mayonnaise.

The "pepper" Columbus found, *Capsicum frutescens*, is unrelated to *piperine*, the black pepper of India. *C. frutescens* is a bushy plant with woody stems that grows in warm and tropical climates. The plant probably originated in the Bolivian Andes, and since many birds can tolerate hot peppers they dispersed the seed throughout Southern and Central America. The plant was domesticated thousands of years before the arrival of Columbus and by the time of his arrival a great many varieties had become adapted to different environments. Plum-like peppers, similar to miniature eggplants, and bright red dagger-like peppers supposedly spiced Montezuma's *chocolatl*, his favorite breakfast drink made from gratings of the Andean cacao bean. Montezuma was however unaware of *piperine*, which he probably would also have enjoyed.

For many years chili was considered a southwestern specialty, although chili con carne has become a popular dish at fast food emporia throughout North America. Recently the chili pepper has enjoyed a popularity boom, and hot salsas have become kitchen favorites. Some Oriental cuisines, like those of the Thai, have become a challenge for enthusiasts because of their intense heat. Posters, kitchen towels, calendars and maps depict chili peppers in every size, color and shape. A recent popular chili pepper calendar lists chilies in alphabetical order starting in January with Anaheim - mild to fairly hot; Ancho—a nutty sweetness when dried; Banana—popular in Creole cooking, etc.

The chili pepper has traveled far and wide; it is a favorite in every part of the world. Last September I was impressed when I saw bright red Jalapeños—a suitable color for their hot character—draped in garlands on the sunny side of almost every dwelling in Turkey. Habañeros, small, waxy and brilliant orange, were favorites in the open markets of Istanbul.

The true chili aficionado finds the cayenne and chili powders available on supermarket shelves insipid. Unadulterated powdered chilies like ancho, mulato or pasilla, can be found in specialty shops and Mexican food stores, but they may not satisfy the dedicated chili-eater. For them, drying, grinding and flaking their own powerful seasonings is essential.

## Drying Chilies

To dry chilies, choose small (the smaller, the hotter) red, <u>mature</u> pods, thread them on a string through the stalks, and hang them in the sun on a south-facing wall. As the chilies dry the pods shrink, become darker, and intensify in flavor. The seeds and membrane become searingly hot and rubber gloves are essential when handling chilies. Core and seed the dried chilies before grinding them into flakes or powder. Some people with cast-iron palates grind them up, seeds and all, and are proud of a cuisine which very few people can tolerate!

The commercial products called red pepper, cayenne, Tabasco sauce, chili powder, chili flakes, paprika, etc. all belong to the *capsicum* family and originated in the Americas. These seasonings are now consumed in larger quantities by more people than any other spice in the entire world.

## The Chili Pepper as Medicine

For thousands of years the Native Americans had accumulated a vast store of knowledge about the plant's medicinal and narcotic effects. It was known to be a general pain-killer and a remedy for colds, asthma and abdominal ailments. Modern medicine confirms many of these health-giving benefits and more. Chilies supply six to nine times the amount of vitamin C found in tomatoes (by weight). They are an excellent source of vitamin A, and are rich in potassium and iron. Modern chili-boosters make near-miraculous claims for a salve made from the alkaloid *capsaicin*, (the active ingredient), which is considered a treatment for shingles and cluster headaches. Recent research indicates that *capsaicin* may stimulate the brain to secrete endorphins, a natural pain killer. It may also bring relief from pain by contracting nerve endings away from painful muscles. *Capsaicin* is also marketed as an anti-mugger device, an alternative to Mace.

Greater health benefits and a richer diversity of food may still lie ahead if researchers explore the chili's ancestral home in the unexplored rain forests, valleys and mountaintops of Central and South America. Ethnobotanists still pursue these studies. They travel to remote villages and look for the old men, the shamans, who administer medicine to the people of their villages. These intrepid ethnobotanists learn the language of their host country, seek out the village medicine men and learn about the plants they skillfully utilize. The botanists carry the plants back to their research laboratory for microbiological analysis. Pharmaceutical companies follow these projects and often finance them. They have been rewarded with new products, and we are all rewarded by the results of this research.

The fierce little red peppers that can deter criminals are equally potent in the kitchen. They can cause serious "burns" and terrible irritations when in contact with skin or eyes. It is important to wear gloves when working with hot chilies.

Fiery pods that can burn your fingers and scorch your throat apparently do not have a similar effect on the digestive tract. Patients with gastro-intestinal diseases, such as hiatus hernia, ulcer, or irritated bowel syndrome, are advised to avoid spicy foods, but spices do not necessarily cause such complaints. *Capsaicin* may actually have beneficial effects on the digestive system by retarding bacterial growth and stimulating peristaltic action. Its anti-bacterial action may reduce the likelihood of gastro-intestinal infection.

Classic salsa originated in Mexico, usually made from combinations of chili peppers, tomatoes and seasonings. In the United States it was considered Southwestern food, the lonesome cowboy's fare. Now it has become an invigorating taste sensation. In many supermarkets bottled salsa outsells ketchup. New versions are sprouting every day, feisty little jalapeño peppers are puréed with milder fruits and vegetables and offer sprightly variations on the salsa theme. Fresh, jaunty tastes and tantalizing flavors enhance low-calorie diets as dips or toppings and eliminate the need for calorie-rich gravies and sauces.

## *Spicy Salsa*
### *The basic recipe*

2 medium-sized ripe tomatoes, seeded and diced

$^1/_2$ medium red onion

1 jalapeño pepper, cored, seeded and diced

Juice of 2 medium limes

1 tablespoon olive oil

Salt (optional)

Freshly ground pepper to taste

Combine ingredients to make about one cup of salsa, which may be safely refrigerated for up to two weeks. Add crushed garlic clove and sprinkle dried basil to the recipe to make it more piquant

## Avocado Salsa

<sup></sup>

$1/4$ cup cider vinegar

1 tablespoon honey

$1/2$ teaspoon ground cumin

$1/4$ teaspoon pepper

1 jalapeño pepper, cored,
   seeded and diced

1 clove garlic, minced

2 avocados, peeled and diced

Combine all ingredients except the avocados, stir, cover and refrigerate. Before serving, stir mixture and add avocados. Toss gently. This salsa glorifies ham, chicken or seafood – or serve as a dip with crackers, tortillas, celery or carrot sticks.

Avocados are known in Mexico as "poor-man's butter." They are not low in calories, but they can be spread thinly and supply that mouth-watering butter taste.

## Mango Salsa

2 mangos, peeled and diced
   small

1 small clove of garlic, minced

1 small jalapeño pepper,
   seeded and minced

2 teaspoons chopped parsley

$1/4$ cup sliced scallions

$1/4$ cup sugar

$1/4$ cup white vinegar

2 tablespoons lime juice

Combine the mangos with garlic, jalapeño and parsley in bowl. Over low heat dissolve the sugar in vinegar. Pour hot vinegar over the mango mixture and stir gently. Add lime juice, cover and refrigerate. Serve with roast pork or lamb and avoid the fat and cholesterol of gravy.

# Sweet Pepper Salsa

1 large red bell pepper

1 large yellow bell pepper

1 large green bell pepper

1 medium jalapeño chili pepper, seeded and finely chopped

4 cloves garlic, roasted peeled and finely chopped

1 cup basil leaves

2 tablespoons olive oil

$1/2$ teaspoon salt

Freshly ground pepper

Roast, peel, seed and devein bell peppers. Chop coarsely. Put all the ingredients into food processor or blender, purée until smooth. Keep in airtight container in refrigerator. Excellent on grilled meat, fish or vegetables and splendid tossed with pasta or rice.

When tomatoes and peppers are plentiful, it is a good idea to prepare and preserve a winter supply of cooked salsa that can be safely stored.

# Cooked Chili Salsa
### *To be bottled and preserved for later use*

1 pound onions

2 pounds fresh mild chili peppers (if you are using jalapeños, reduce quantity to 8 peppers, unless you love foods very HOT)

5 pounds tomatoes

3 teaspoons salt

$1/2$ teaspoon pepper

$3/4$ cup cider vinegar

Coarsely grind onions and chili peppers. Peel tomatoes and chop into small pieces. Combine onion, peppers and tomatoes, add remaining ingredients. Heat and simmer for ten minutes. Pack into clean, hot jars. Leave $1/4$ inch headroom. Seal and process 15 minutes in simmering hot water bath, or pack in rigid freezer containers. Heat before serving.

Cowboys, pioneers and adventurers trekking across uncharted lands believed in a chili mystique; a man could prove his hardihood by the intensity of the heat he could swallow. Writers of western tales called chili the "pemmican of the Southwest." The chili mystique is kept alive throughout the southwest by annual "chili cook-outs". Strict tradition dictates that chili must be cooked slowly in a heavy open pot. It must not be steamed or stewed and the fat must not be removed during cooking. When cooled, the fat may be removed. A prize-winning recipe is expected to observe the rules and generate plenty of "heat" and this recent winner observed the traditions (I don't know the author of this recipe; it was handed out at a State Fair I attended many years ago in Texas).

# Southwestern Prize-winning Chili Con Carne

2 medium onions, chopped fine

2 cloves garlic, minced

2 tablespoon vegetable oil

5 ounces hot chili powder

1 tablespoon regular chili powder

3 pounds lean ground beef

3 ounces sausage meat

1 cup beef broth

$2^1/_2$ cups cooked kidney beans

2 jalapeño peppers, seeded and minced

2 tablespoons ground cumin

12 ounces tomato sauce, canned or homemade

1 tablespoon oregano, steeped in $^1/_2$ cup boiling water to make a tea

Salt to taste

In a large Dutch oven sauté onions and garlic in oil. Stir in chili powders, mix thoroughly, and cook for about 3 minutes. In a separate skillet brown the meat in small batches, do not crowd pan. Add browned meat to the onions. Add half the beef broth and kidney beans to mixture. Sauté sausage and jalapeño chili in skillet, add cumin, tomato sauce, oregano and rest of broth. Add to meat and cook uncovered for two hours or until meat is tender. Stir frequently. Add water as needed. (It takes a good deal of water.) After cooking, refrigerate chili and remove fat. Chili should be reheated over a slow fire, with frequent stirrings to prevent scorching.

In some areas of Texas the beans are omitted, in fact they are considered absolutely forbidden in some parts of the state.

Vegetable chili defies tradition but this dish tastes like the real thing and is better suited to healthful guidelines.

## No-meat Chili

1 pound plum tomatoes

2 tablespoons vegetable oil

2 large onions, chopped

3 large cloves of garlic, minced

1 jalapeño pepper, minced

1 green pepper, minced

2 cups tomato purée

$1/4$ teaspoon coriander

$1/8$ teaspoon allspice

$1 1/2$ teaspoons oregano

1 tablespoon mild chili powder

$1 1/2$ teaspoons cumin

$1/2$ pound dried pinto or kidney beans, thoroughly cooked ( or two 16 ounce cans)

Chop half the tomatoes, purée the rest. Sauté onion, garlic and green pepper and jalapeño in hot oil until onion is soft but not brown. Add tomatoes, puréed and chopped, spices and beans. Tasty additions are sliced mushrooms, diced zucchini or eggplant and crumbled tofu. Simmer chili about 30 minutes. Will make four to five servings.

Another version of a meatless-chili uses *capsicum* in sweet pepper, chili, paprika and cayenne. This spicy dish may be refrigerated and reheated without losing flavor.

# Meatless Chili

4 cups black beans

2 tablespoons cumin seed

1 tablespoon oregano

1 teaspoon sage

2 medium onions, chopped

1 large green pepper, seeded and chopped

2 cloves garlic, minced

$^1/_4$ cup olive oil

1 teaspoon cayenne pepper

1 tablespoon paprika

1 teaspoon salt

3 cups canned Italian plum tomatoes, puréed

$^1/_2$ cup bottled jalapeño slices, minced

Grated Cheddar cheese

Chopped cilantro or parsley

Soak the beans overnight, drain, discard and replace the water and cook beans until tender. Drain, saving a cup of the pot water.

In a small pan over medium heat, sprinkle cumin seed, oregano and sage to release the natural flavor. Set aside. Heat oil, add onions, green pepper, garlic and the toasted herbs. When the onions are soft, add the tomato purée, jalapeños, the cooked beans and the cup of pot liquid. Add the salt, paprika and the cayenne gradually. Simmer for at least 30 minutes, adding liquid if needed. Add cheese and cilantro when ready to serve.

# Turkey Chili
## *A low-fat, low cholesterol recipe*

1 pound freshly ground turkey (thawed frozen turkey may be used)

1 medium sized onion, coarsely chopped

1 green pepper, seeded and coarsely chopped

1 medium jalapeño pepper, seeded and chopped

1 clove of garlic, minced

3 cups of chicken broth, canned or homemade

$2^1/_2$ cups pinto beans, thoroughly cooked or canned

2 cans (28–ounce) crushed tomatoes

1 can (6–ounce) tomato paste

3 tablespoons chili powder (reduce to 2 if home-dried)

2 teaspoons cumin

2 bay leaves

$1/_8$ teaspoon salt

$1/_8$ teaspoon pepper

Brush a large Dutch oven lightly with salad oil or coat with cooking spray. Over medium heat stir turkey until it crumbles and turns light brown. Drain turkey in colander to remove all fat. Wipe the pot dry and lightly brush with oil. Sauté onion, green pepper, jalapeño pepper and garlic over medium heat until vegetables are tender. Add the turkey and stir. Pour in chicken broth add beans, tomatoes, tomato paste, chili powder, cumin, bay leaves, salt and pepper. Bring to a boil, simmer for one hour, stirring occasionally. Remove bay leaves and serve while chili is piping hot. Serve with bread, rice or other grains.

Liquids don't quench the fire of chili; they spread the heat to other parts of the mouth. Grains on the other hand absorb the heat and spread the flavor.

\* \* \*

In 1498 Vasco de Gama rounded the Cape of Good Hope and reached the Asian subcontinent. Portuguese traders followed his sea-route and brought the chili pepper to India. It was eagerly accepted by oriental cooks, and India now produces more chili peppers than the true peppercorns which had once been the envy of the world. Some of India's most traditional curries now combine chili with cumin and other Oriental spices for complex new tastes. Szechuan and Hunan cooking, famous for the heat they generate, make liberal use of chilies. Thailand also has a voracious appetite for chilies. Thai specialties go from sizzling to blazing.

# Oriental Chicken Salad

1¹/₂ cups cooked chicken, shredded or cut into bite-sized pieces

2 celery stalks

2 small red chili peppers, minced with seeds

1 tablespoon finely minced ginger root or 1 teaspoon ground ginger

2 cloves garlic, finely minced

2 scallions, white part only, minced

2 tablespoons light soy sauce

2 tablespoons vinegar

1 teaspoon sugar

¹/₄ teaspoon freshly ground white pepper

2 tablespoons sesame oil or peanut oil

Cut the celery thinly on the diagonal; stack and cut into matchstick shreds. Parboil for 10 seconds, drain, cool under cold water, and drain again.

Mix chilies, ginger, garlic and scallions with soy sauce, vinegar, sugar, salt and pepper. Toss the chicken with celery and oil and combine with chili mixture. Let stand for ten minutes to blend. Serve at room temperature.

# Szechuan Pork

2¹/₂ tablespoons dark soy sauce

1¹/₂ tablespoons light soy sauce

3 tablespoons chicken or vegetable stock

1 tablespoon tomato paste

2 tablespoons chili sauce (see below)

1 tablespoon sugar

## Sauce

2¹/₂ tablespoons dark soy sauce

1¹/₂ tablespoons light soy sauce

3 tablespoons chicken or vegetable stock

1 tablespoon tomato paste

2 tablespoons chili sauce (see below)

1 tablespoon sugar

Place pork in large saucepan and cover with water. Bring to boil, reduce heat and simmer for 30 minutes. Let pork cool in water for another 30 minutes. Remove, drain and slice pork very thin. Slice onion thinly and dice peppers. Seed and shred chilies and cut green onions into 2-inch pieces.

Heat the oil in a wok or skillet. When oil is hot but not smoking, stir-fry onion for 1 minute, add pork and stir-fry for 2 minutes. Stir in sauce and bring to a boil. Add peppers, green onions and chilies and stir for another 2 minutes. Serves 4 or 6.

* * *

Hot barbeque sauces are a commercial staple, but homemade chili sauce belongs in a different class. It is lighter and livelier, and its fresh flavor invigorates marinades and sauces. It adds a new dimension as a topping for steaks and hamburgers and is well worth the trouble of putting it together and keeping it on hand.

# Chili-Pepper Sauce

4 large ripe tomatoes

1 dozen hot red peppers— ripe Jalapeños are hot enough

2 cups vinegar, divided

1 teaspoon salt

$1/2$ cup sugar

Cheesecloth bag containing 1 tablespoon pickling spice

Chop the tomatoes coarsely and combine with the peppers and 1 cup vinegar. Boil in a large pot or kettle until vegetables are soft. Strain the vegetables through a food mill to remove seeds and skin. Return purée to the kettle, add the second cup of vinegar, salt, sugar and the pickling spice bag. Bring to a boil then simmer slowly until the sauce thickens. Remove spice bag and pour hot sauce into hot jars, leaving $1/4$–inch head space. Refrigerate when cool, or adjust lids on hot canning jars to process in hot water bath for 10 minutes. Makes two pints. Steak, meatloaf and hamburgers sizzle when topped with this sauce.

## Chili Oil - a secret helper

Many cookbooks suggest adding oil to water in which pasta is cooked. I've never found this effective in keeping pasta strands separate because the oil rises to the top and is drained away before it can coat the strands. A little oil tossed on pasta after it is drained keeps strands separate and easy to manage. Flavored oil adds another dimension to the taste. Guests often ask "what makes the pasta so good?" The answer is that chili oil is subtly adding flavor to the pasta.

Heat two cups of peanut or salad oil in a sauce pan. Stir in $1/4$ cup dried chili pepper flakes. Remove from heat, cool, store in covered jar at room temperature for about two weeks so that the flavor reaches its peak. Check from time to time to see whether the spiced oil suits your taste.

## Chili Garlic Oil

Separate and peel the cloves in one whole head of garlic (put the entire head into boiling water and let it steep for 2 minutes, remove from water, then the cloves will be easier to separate and peel). In a saucepan add garlic cloves to 2 cups olive oil. Bring to a boil, turn down heat and simmer until garlic turns golden brow, 10 to 15 minutes. Let cool, then add 1 tablespoon chili flakes. Let stand for at least a day before using. This oil needs to be refrigerated because garlic may have vestiges of live bacteria from the soil.

## Bell Peppers - the friendlier capsicum

Bell peppers—green, red, orange or yellow—are a gentler, milder form of *capsicum*. Hot or cold, sliced, sautéed, roasted or pickled, they are a wonderful vegetable that adds color, texture and vitamin C to every dish.

Bell peppers are mechanically harvested (most chilies still have to be hand-picked); they grow in many parts of the country and are available throughout the year. Green bell peppers are Florida's second largest crop and they are at their best during the winter months when other vegetables may be in short supply. Red, yellow and orange peppers are the fully-ripe varieties. They are sweeter, more decorative, and more expensive. They stay in the ground longer, which entails later harvesting, extended land use and greater care in handling. The long tapered green peppers, sometimes called Italian peppers, have a thinner texture and a gentle taste suited to mild sauces, and they are a good substitute for ripe peppers.

Peppers are plentiful, inexpensive, and well worth freezing in season—especially the red ones—the price drops as the season tapers off. Choose peppers that are plump and shiny. Wrinkled or wilted peppers lose vitamins as well as flavor and are never a bargain.

**To freeze whole peppers,** cut peppers—green or red—in half, remove the stem, discard the seeds, cut into strips and pack in plastic bags without blanching or peeling.

Puréed peppers have a velvety smoothness when mixed with a few drops of oil, almost the texture of a buttery sauce. Chefs looking for ways to cut down on fats blend spices with the puréed peppers to thicken gravies and achieve some splendid tastes. Peppers need to be free of their skin and must be peeled. If the purée is to be frozen it should be stored in rigid containers.

**To peel peppers,** char the peppers by turning them on the tines of a long fork over a grill, an open flame on a gas stove, or under a hot broiler, about one inch from heat. Turn frequently until peppers are charred on all sides. Put them in a paper bag for about ten minutes to cool. The steam releases the skin which peels off easily when the peppers are cool enough to handle. Rub with a paper towel to remove charred bits. Do not rinse.

# *Puréed Peppers*

2 large bell peppers, the red
   are handsome

1 or 2 tablespoons olive oil

2 cloves garlic, minced

6 ounces canned tomato
   paste

Salt and pepper to taste

Remove seeds and stems from peeled peppers, cut into strips and combine with other ingredients. Purée in blender or food processor. Makes $1^1/_2$ cups of purée.

Bell peppers and chilies arrived in North Africa soon after their introduction in Spain, and from Morocco comes this smooth and spicy salad.

# *Pepper Salad*

3 peppers—2 green, 1 red

$^1/_2$ teaspoon salt

1 teaspoon cumin

2 tablespoon freshly
   squeezed lemon juice

2 tablespoons olive oil

1 tablespoon peanut oil

$^1/_4$ teaspoon ground hot
   chili

2 teaspoons chopped fresh
   parsley

Dice peeled peppers into $^1/_2$ inch cubes; add salt, cumin, lemon juice, oils and chili. Mix well. Garnish with chopped parsley.

# Marinated Pepper

3 green or red bell peppers

3 long Italian peppers

2 cloves garlic, minced

2 tablespoons lemon juice

1 teaspoon wine vinegar

3 tablespoons of olive oil

$1/2$ teaspoon cumin

1 teaspoon salt

$1/4$ teaspoon pepper

Split the peppers in half. Remove the stems and scrape out the seeds. Cut into $1/2$ inch strips. Mix remaining ingredients and pour over peppers. Refrigerate. Add marinated peppers to salads or serve on lettuce for antipasto. The marinated strips make a delightful garnish for rice or pasta. Makes 2 $1/2$ cups.

# Red Pepper Sauce
*Enlivens bland food*

1 medium onion, coarsely chopped

1 tablespoon olive oil

1 clove garlic, minced

3 red peppers, peeled and coarsely chopped or 15-ounce can of red peppers or pimientos

2 drops Tabasco Sauce (member of the vitamin-rich capsicum family)

Slowly sauté the onion in hot olive oil until soft, add garlic and peppers and cook until mixture is soft and free of moisture. Purée in blender or food processor; stir in Tabasco sauce. This makes about $2/3$ cup and can be spooned into pan juices for thickened flavorful gravies or spaghetti sauce.

Blends well in pizza.

# Chicken Adobo with Peppers
## *A Cuban delicacy*

2 tablespoons lime juice

1 tablespoon minced jalapeño pepper

2 teaspoons olive oil

1 clove garlic, minced

4 boned, skinned chicken breast halves

1 green bell pepper, cut into ½ inch slices

1 red bell pepper, cut into $^1/_2$ inch slices

Combine lime juice, jalapeño pepper, oil and garlic in a bowl, stir well, add chicken breast halves and turn them so that they are covered with marinade. Cover, refrigerate for about 2 hours, turning occasionally.

Coat a large nonstick skillet with cooking spray or coat a non-stick pan with a teaspoon of oil. Heat pan and add bell peppers, sauté 3 minutes. Remove bell peppers from skillet, set aside. Add chicken and marinade to skillet, cook until lightly browned on both sides. Return bell peppers to skillet, cover and cook an additional 5 minutes or until chicken is done. Serve over rice. Makes 4 portions.

Italian peppers often accompany tomatoes, but here they stand alone as an attractive and spicy sauce for pasta.

# Venetian Pepperoni Sauce for Pasta

$1^1/_2$ pounds green peppers, finely chopped

2 onions, finely chopped

$^1/_4$ cup parsley, chopped

2 cloves garlic, minced

$^1/_4$ cup olive oil

$2^1/_2$ tablespoons wine vinegar

4 teaspoons sugar

Salt and freshly ground pepper to taste

Heat the oil in a heavy saucepan and add all the vegetables, salt and pepper. Cover and simmer, stirring occasionally, for one hour.

Stir in the vinegar and sugar and simmer 15 minutes longer. Purée the sauce in a food processor or blender. Check seasoning and return sauce to the saucepan to heat slowly. This is enough sauce for $1^1/_2$ pounds of spaghetti or other pasta.

Paprika comes from the dried pods of *Capsicum tetragona* (the bonnet pepper), which is particularly rich in vitamins C and A. Columbus brought the plant to Spain and it traveled eastward across the Mediterranean when the Ottoman Empire held sway. In 1526 the Turks invaded Hungary and brought the ground bonnet peppers to its subject peoples. Paprika became Hungary's national condiment, and one of their most popular and traditional dishes is Paprikaš (pronounced paprika<u>sh</u>). Albert von Szent-Gygorgyi, a Hungarian scientist, received the 1937 Nobel Prize for the discovery of ascorbic acid (vitamin C) and it seems fitting that his research identified peppers as a source of the vitamin.

Paprika may be sweet, mild or hot. A few sprinkles can color and flavor an entire dish. Paprika burns when subjected to prolonged intense heat, and is best added after the other ingredients have been browned.

## Chicken Paprikaš
### Classic Hungarian recipe

1 broiler, cut into 8 pieces

2 tablespoon olive oil

1 medium–sized onion

1 clove of garlic

2 tablespoon sweet paprika

1/4 pound fresh mushrooms, cleaned and thickly sliced

1 green bell pepper

1 bay leaf

1 cup canned plum tomatoes—reserve liquid

1 cup water or chicken broth mixed with tomato liquid

2 tablespoons flour

1/2 cup sour cream

Heat olive oil in large, heavy skillet. Rinse chicken, and pat dry. Sauté chicken lightly, a few pieces at a time. Transfer chicken to casserole and pour off all but 2 tablespoons of fat. Sauté onion in fat, add paprika, garlic, mushrooms, green pepper and bay leaf. Stir until blended. Add tomatoes and water. Pour sauce over chicken, cover and simmer gently for about an hour, or until chicken is tender. Transfer chicken to a warm serving dish, discard bay leaf. Bring sauce to a boil. Dissolve flour in cupful of hot sauce, add sour cream and more sauce, stir and then gently add the mixture to remaining sauce, stirring until sauce is blended. Pour sauce over chicken and serve with rice or dumplings. You can eliminate calories by leaving out the gravy and sour cream. Just reduce liquid to about half or until it thickens.

During the depression years potatoes were cheap and my family groaned about too many "spuds" or "taters," except when we had potatoes paprikaš. In spite of her frugal ways, my mother bought real paprika - imported from Hungary by Paprikas-Weiss, the store that had spices to make the senses reel. It was a wonderland with wooden tubs overflowing with colorful dried beans, kasha, and lentils. Pasta came in every size, shape and color. Glass containers displayed caraway, pumpkin, sunflower, poppy and other seeds. With a handsome little scoop the clerk weighed out small quantities of cinnamon, cloves, nutmeg or paprika which he then stuffed into little blue-paper cones. In the subway, on our way home, people sniffed the air to identify the spicy fragrances.

## *Potatoes Paprikaš*

2 tablespoons butter or margarine

1 small onion, finely chopped

6 potatoes (preferably red, waxy) cooked in skins, peeled and cut into $1/4$ inch slices

$1/2$ teaspoon salt, or to taste

$1^1/2$ teaspoons paprika

Melt butter or margarine in skillet, add the onion and sauté for about 3 minutes until soft but not burned. Add potatoes, salt and paprika, keep heat on high to brown the potatoes, but stir often to prevent burning. The paprika will not burn with such quick browning. Serves six as a side dish or three as a vegetable entree.

In the spring of 1535 the fearsome Barbarossa with a small contingent of Turkish ships stormed his way into the African port of Tunis and made it a base from which he could intercept merchant fleets passing from the western to the eastern Mediterranean. The Spaniards, Germans and Portuguese launched a mighty armada and recaptured the city, only to cede it to the Turks in a later campaign. Tunis was the 16th century bridge linking east and west. During a turbulent century of warfare, it was a major point for bringing foods from the new world into Austria, Hungary, Germany and Africa. In commemoration of its significant role, here is a recipe from Tunis.

## Peppers and Eggs Tunisian Style

2 large red or green peppers, seeded and sliced into $1/2$ inch strips

2 onions, thinly sliced

1 clove garlic, finely minced

2 ripe tomatoes, peeled, seeded and coarsely chopped

2 tablespoons vegetable oil

4 eggs

Salt and pepper to taste

Heat oil in skillet, sauté onions and peppers for 10 minutes, until soft. Add garlic, tomatoes, salt and pepper. Cook over medium heat for another 5 or 10 minutes until liquid is absorbed.

Preheat oven to 350 degrees. Lightly grease four individual oven-proof dishes, divide vegetable mixture among them. Drop an egg into each dish and bake for ten minutes until the eggs have set. Serves four.

# 5

# A Story of Corn

On the paved road to Teotitlan del Camino, about 29 miles southeast of Tehuacán in the valley of Mexico, stands a small, unpretentious museum with corn as its major exhibit. The display starts with a tiny corn cob, no larger than a cigarette stub. That tiny specimen is more than 5000 years old, but the corn story probably goes back 7000 years. By the time Columbus reached the New World, corn supported civilizations, played a key role in many religious beliefs, and was the object of adulation as an Earth Goddess. Corn is like no other grain, and it is still almost miraculous in its adaptability and versatility. At the present time corn is second only to wheat in worldwide production and it is the most prolific crop in history.

One grass, *teosinte*, is believed to have been the parent stock from which the plant was created, but the plant is so changed from any ancestral form that it can never revert to its wild state. Microbiological research seems to confirm *teosinte* as its origin, but ongoing scientific investigations continue to be a source of interest to archeologists, botanists and geneticists. One famous ethnobotanist says "Corn is probably the most remarkable plant-breeding accomplishment of all time."

In the New World it became adapted to every region and every need. Plant-breeders raised overflowing crops of flint corn, sweet corn, dent corn, popcorn and corn for grinding. The silk from one variety was fertilized with the pollen of another type to create hundreds of races or varieties adapted to a wide range of geography. In rain forests (with 100 or more inches of annual precipitation) and in areas which received no more than five inches of rain per year, it still supported populations that developed traditions, systems of government and religious beliefs. The plant was worshipped as "The Sacred Mother", the giver of life.

The Taino Indians called the plant *mahez,* the botanical name is *Zea mays*, and only in America does "corn" specifically refer to the plant as we know it. "Corn" elsewhere is a generic term that denotes the prevalent grain of any country. In England it means wheat, in Scotland or Ireland it means oats. Throughout most of the world and in almost every language the plant is called maize. We shall continue to call it corn because we are accustomed to American usage.

In addition to corn, the Native Americans planted beans and squash on mounds they called milpahs. In the Yucatan you can still find milpah agriculture where the tall corn stalk supports the climbing beans and the spiny growth of squash keeps weeds down and discourages animal predation. The plants were called the "The Three Sisters of Life." Modern food scientists agree that these are life-enhancing plants. They sustain life by providing the twenty amino acids needed for complete protein synthesis. Some time ago I came across a recipe reputed to be of ancient origin—I forget where I saw it, but it now resides in my box of recipe cards. It contains spices not native to the American continents, but spices were exchanged early in the history of food in the New World.

# *The Three Sisters Casserole*

1 cup dried pinto or kidney beans

$^1/_8$ teaspoon chili powder

$^1/_8$ teaspoon cayenne powder

1 teaspoon cumin

1 clove garlic, minced

1 cup diced onion

$^2/_3$ cup diced squash

3 cups of fresh corn cut from cob

1 cup red and green bell peppers, diced

1 pinch salt

Soak the beans overnight, drain the water, rinse and add $3^1/_2$ cups fresh water together with the chili and cayenne peppers. Bring beans to a boil and simmer for one hour. In another pan sauté the garlic, onion, peppers, cumin and another pinch of cayenne, until onions are soft. Add the squash and cook until tender, about 15 minutes. Add corn and cook for another ten minutes. Season with salt and mix corn casserole and beans together. Garnish with strips of scallion.

The paleo-Indians had never seen a horse, cow or sheep before the god-like Spanish conquistadores, fitted out with steel armor and weapons, arrived on horseback. They were dismayed when sacred corn was fed to the Spaniards' beasts, but Spanish tradition exalted the powerful animals that constituted food, wealth, and bravery. Men who pitted their strength against the power of the bull were glorified and no food was too sacred for El Toro.

In the 16th century, when the Ottoman Empire at the height of its power seized control of the eastern Mediterranean, it thrust its naval power as far as the Danube valley and the Turks almost reached Vienna before fierce fighting held them from taking the city. The Viennese and most of Eastern Europe were exhausted and famine-ridden after the long siege.

The Turks were wheat-eaters, disdainful of the corn that had been taken from Spanish and Portuguese galleons as spoils of war. The Hungarians and Romanians, defeated and hungry, embraced the new food. They called it by the Portuguese name *milho grosso,* because they believed it to be a native grain of Portugal. *Mamaliga*, cornmeal pudding, became the national dish of the Romanian people.

## Mamaliga (Cornmeal Pudding)

4 cups water

1 teaspoon salt

2 cups yellow cornmeal

3 tablespoons butter or
   margarine

Bring water to a boil, gradually stir in cornmeal, reduce heat to medium, but continue stirring until mixture thickens—about three minutes. Stir in butter, turn heat down to low. Cover and let simmer for another 20 minutes. The pudding is done when it no longer sticks to side of pan when stirred.

Lightly grease a wooden cutting board and spoon the cooked mamaliga onto the surface. Let it rest for about a minute, then with a knife or the back of spoon dipped in cold water, mold the mamaliga into an oval mound. To slice it in the Romanian style, cut a piece of thread about 20 inches long, stretch the thread tightly between your hands, and pull down through the mounded pudding, cutting off slices. Or be untraditional and just use a knife!

Serve hot with grated cheese, or dip in Parmesan cheese and fry in butter or margarine until browned on both sides.

Turkish ships brought corn to conquered Italian and north African ports. In the 16th century corn gruel became an African staple. The Italians made a cornmeal pudding called "polenta" that is still almost as popular as pasta.

# Basic Polenta

6 cups water

1 teaspoon salt

2 cups polenta flour or coarse-ground yellow cornmeal

3 or 4 tablespoons of butter or margarine

In a large pot or double boiler, bring the salted water to a boil. To avoid lumps add cornmeal very, very slowly and stir constantly for five or ten minutes. Then let simmer slowly for another 20 minutes, stirring occasionally. Or put over hot, but not boiling, water in double boiler and let cook until cornmeal separates from the sides of the pan easily.

Cubes of Fontina cheese and a sprinkling of Parmesan make this a rich savory accompaniment to a meal. Cooled, sliced and fried or grilled, it is a good side dish. It can be cubed and added to soup or served with gravy.

In Verona polenta is served with a delicious sausage gravy.

# Polenta with Sausage Gravy

1 pound Italian sausage or sausage links

2 tablespoons water

1 small onion, chopped

1 clove garlic, minced

1 medium can stewed tomatoes

1 medium can tomato purée

Place sausage in large saucepan with 2 tablespoons water. Prick sausage and let brown in its own fat. Drain fat and just leave the pan somewhat oily. Add onion, garlic, and salt, if desired, or add minced jalapeño pepper instead of salt. Brown mixture, stir and add the tomatoes and tomato purée. Simmer for about $1^1/_2$ hours. Pour the sauce over freshly cooked polenta and arrange sausage around the platter. Or fry cooled sliced polenta and cover with sauce, and sausage.

## The Emergence of Pellagara and the Loss of Corn's Popularity in Europe

Corn became a basic grain for Europeans and Africans who could not afford expensive wheat products. In southern parts of the United States, corn was food for sharecroppers and tenant farmers. It was always cheaper than grain starches. A short growing season made it economical and it did not need to be threshed, winnowed or flailed. It could be readily milled into versatile cornmeal. But wherever it became a diet staple of a country, a dreadful disease attacked the corn-eaters. This disease became epidemic in Africa, Spain, Egypt and France and attacked southern sharecroppers in the USA. It caused ugly skin lesions, violent gastric upsets, mental confusion and dreadful neurological derangements. An Italian doctor named the disease "pellagra" (bad skin), but it was popularly called "mealies" from the original Portuguese name *milho grosso*. The cause of the disease was not identified for hundreds of years and in Europe the popularity of corn waned.

In the 1920s, the vitamin niacin was identified, and pellagra was found to be a vitamin-deficiency disease. Corn is high in protein, but, unlike other grains, lacks both niacin and the amino acid tryptophan which the body uses to synthesize vitamins. Pellagra, today no longer a medical threat except in isolated areas where vitamin-enriched cornmeal is not available, has left many Europeans with a feeling that corn is primarily hog and cattle feed. In Africa cornmeal mush, still called "mealies," is eaten with greens, and is a basic food. Corn in its many guises has worldwide distribution but fresh sweet corn is an American delicacy. *Le Drugstore* near L'Etoile in Paris advertises fresh sweet corn flown in from the USA at the height of its summer season, and we met some Frenchmen who had driven from Brittany to Paris to savor this rare treat. We sent them seed for their garden when we returned to the States.

How is it that pellagra did not decimate the pre-Columbian Americans? It is a story of primitive technology working with Nature. Cornmeal for tortillas and other dishes is made by grinding corn kernels into "masa". To soften the kernels, destroy the hulls, and make grinding easier, Indian women soaked the corn overnight in water to which they added wood ash. They ground the corn with manos (pestles) in stone metates. Not until the twentieth century did food scientists discover that wood ash contains alkali that chemically changes corn into a form that releases niacin and makes protein available to the body. Mechanical milling and grinding eliminated the need to soften the corn by soaking it in wood ash, thus causing a niacin deficiency disease, the dreaded pellagra.

* * *

Corn with hulls too thick to grind and too tough to chew is still soaked in lime, lye or wood ash, alkalis that eat away the hulls without damaging the pulp. Kernels removed from treated cobs are dried and made into hominy, a word that comes from "*uskatahomen*" in the Algonquian language. Grits are ground hominy kernels.

The wood ash that American Indians added to corn before grinding bleached the corn and added the subtle flavor of cedar, juniper or hickory woods. A pinch of wood ash is still added to many Native American dishes, more as a ritual observance than as a flavor enhancer, but the habit persists and the ritual is cherished.

Corn's major requirement for growth is water. Nevertheless the Hopi people have been growing high-yield blue corn in the southwest desert for two hundred years. Blue corn is a low-growing plant that wastes no water or energy on elaborate foliage. Agronomists are now studying the growing technique to see whether blue corn can be adapted to other arid soils. It may save people in Ethiopia and the Sudan from periodic famine and starvation.

Blue corn is known as "*masa harina*" among the Hopi people. It is held in high esteem for its healthful attributes. Blue corn flour is now a health food store item, it is sold as a mix for pancakes, tortillas and other cornmeal treats.

## Blue Corn Tortillas

1 quart boiling water

1 tablespoon butter or other fat

4 cups blue corn flour (Masa harina)

Add boiling water to corn and fat, stir and mix until all the corn is moistened. Grease a flat grill or frying pan. Moisten hands and make flat patties about 6 inches in diameter. Fry, turn and stack when cooked through. Makes 12 tortillas.

Grains and legumes combined make complex non-animal proteins. Native people introduced succotash, a combination of beans and corn, to the early colonists and this helped them survive.

Succotash was once a restaurant staple, the vegetable that came out of a can in hash houses and truck stops. Now succotash made with fresh sweet corn and beans is embellished with chili peppers, tomatoes, herbs, bits of broccoli or cauliflower and it has become a prestigious dish.

Corn reached Asia some time between 1520 and 1560 at a time when hungry peasants were ready to revolt. Portuguese seamen rounded the horn of Africa and reached China with seed corn in time to save the Chinese dynasty from revolution. Corn still constitutes about 25% of China's grain harvest and cornstarch gives Chinese sauces a velvety texture. But fresh corn is not as prestigious as rice or wheat, and corn is not a major ingredient in Chinese cooking except for "baby corn," tiny, soft ears grown for the luxury market. This stir-fry recipe can be made with cooked corn kernels of fresh sweet corn.

# Stir-Fried Chicken with Corn

1 whole chicken breast, cut into
$^1/_4$ inch cubes

$^1/_2$ teaspoon salt

1 tablespoon cornstarch

1 egg white

2 tablespoons vegetable oil

$^1/_4$ pound snow peas

$^1/_4$ pound canned bamboo
shoots, diced (optional)

1 cup baby corn or corn kernels
from freshly cooked sweet
corn

1 cup button mushrooms or $^1/_2$
pound sliced fresh
mushrooms

## Sauce

1 tablespoon light soy sauce

$^1/_2$ cup chicken stock

$^1/_2$ teaspoon sugar

2 tablespoons sherry or white
wine

1 tablespoon cornstarch
blended with 3 tablespoons
water

Salt and pepper to taste

Rub chicken lightly with salt, dust with cornstarch and coat with egg white. Heat oil in wok or fry-pan. When oil is hot but not smoking, stir-fry chicken for about 30 seconds. Add snow peas, bamboo shoots, corn and mushrooms and stir-fry over medium heat for another minute. Combine sauce ingredients and add to chicken. Stir and turn together for about 1 minute until boiling and thickened.

In the United States less than 1% of the corn crop is eaten as fresh sweet corn. Animal feed, corn syrup, cornmeal, soft drinks, additives, paper and plastics products, even soaps and insecticides have corn as the essential ingredient.

Corn on the cob, a summer delight, is sweet as sugar when it is fresh but the sugar quickly turns to starch after harvesting. Florida geneticists have now bred a sweet corn called "Supersweet" which converts sugar to starch more slowly and can be shipped to distant markets. But freshly picked corn is a special treat.

Corn cobs with green, tight husks are usually freshest. They should be kept in refrigerated bins in the store and refrigerated with the husks intact at home. Corn with husks removed, or partially removed, should be refrigerated in a perforated plastic bag. The natural conversion of sugar into starch can be slowed by parboiling shucked ears for two minutes before refrigeration or freezing. When ready to serve, drop the parboiled corn into boiling unsalted water, cover, turn off the heat and let steam for five minutes. A pinch of sugar in the water enhances the taste, but do not add salt because it toughens the corn. Cooking time for fresh corn varies—five minutes in boiling water is usually all it takes.

To microwave corn, wrap individual ears in wax paper and microwave on high for 3 to 5 minutes. Or stack ears in a microwavable dish with 3 tablespoons of water and microwave on high for 5 to 7 minutes.

To roast corn, pull back the husk and remove the silk, then replace the husk, tie the ends with cotton string or strip of husk, and soak in enough water to cover for 10 minutes. Bury corn in coals of a barbecue or place on top of a grill and turn occasionally for 15 minutes.

Corn comes in white, yellow and "butter and egg" varieties which are mixed yellow and white. All are rich in vitamin C, but the yellow also has beta carotene, the precursor of vitamin A, a valuable food resource.

Leftover corn combined with meat or vegetables is hearty, satisfying food. Appetizers, soups, side dishes entrees are all made more cheerful with sweet chewy kernels of corn.

Here is a soup that can be served as a main course. If you cannot use the entire quantity right away, add as many shrimps as you think you will eat at one sitting, and if some soup is left over you can just add more fresh shrimp to make a good encore.

# Corn and Shrimp Soup

3 tablespoons unsalted butter or margarine—or if you like, $1/4$ cup bacon drippings

2 tablespoons all-purpose flour

1 cup chopped celery

1 cup chopped green pepper

1 cup chopped onion

1 clove minced garlic

2 teaspoons salt

$1/2$ teaspoon pepper

1 teaspoon dried thyme

1 can (16 ounce) whole tomatoes, undrained and chopped, or an equivalent quantity of fresh tomatoes

1 (6-ounce) can tomato paste

3 cups corn kernels about 6 ears

2 pounds fresh medium shrimp, peeled, deveined and cut in half, or 1-pound package of frozen shrimp

Place butter or bacon drippings along with flour in your largest Dutch oven. Cook over medium heat until roux is browning, then add celery, green pepper, onion, garlic, salt, pepper and thyme. Stir the vegetables into the roux and cook, uncovered, until softened, about ten minutes. (Roux is a mixture of flour and butter browned together—the basic ingredients for thickening gravy, soups or stew.)

Add tomatoes, tomato paste, water and corn. Bring to a boil; reduce heat and simmer uncovered, 45 minutes. Stir in shrimp, simmer uncovered for 10 minutes. This will make almost a gallon of delicious soup.

Other variations on the same corn theme are also delectable.

# Curried Corn Soup

2 cups corn kernels (about 4 ears of cooked corn)

1 tablespoon unsalted butter

1 cup finely chopped onion

1 tablespoon curry powder

2 tablespoons flour

1 large apple, peeled and coarsely chopped or grated

4 cups unsalted chicken broth

1 bay leaf

1 cup plain yogurt

Sauté onion and garlic in butter. Stir in curry powder and flour. Add apple, chicken broth and bay leaf. Simmer for about 20 minutes. Remove bay leaf, pour soup into food processor or blender and process until smooth. Reheat and add corn, bring to a boil. Remove from heat and stir in yogurt.

# Corn and Zucchini Casserole

3 cups of fresh corn kernels cut from cob—about 6 ears

3 medium zucchini

1 onion, thinly sliced

1 clove garlic, minced

1 tomato, peeled, seeded

2 tablespoons vegetable oil

1 tablespoon unsalted butter

$^1/_2$ cup grated sharp cheddar cheese

Salt and pepper to taste

Heat oil and sauté zucchini, onion and garlic for ten minutes or until tender. Add tomatoes, corn, salt and pepper, stir, and let simmer for five minutes. Spoon the vegetables into a buttered baking dish, then sprinkle with cheese and dot with butter. Bake for 15 minutes or until cheese has melted. This is a good vegetarian main dish. Serves 4.

# Corn and Cheese Custard

1 tablespoon butter

1 onion, chopped

1 sweet red pepper, chopped

3 cups cooked fresh sweet corn—about 6 ears

2 teaspoons fresh parsley, minced

1$^1/_2$ cups milk

2 eggs

1$^1/_2$ cup grated sharp cheddar cheese

Salt and pepper to taste

Sauté onion and pepper in butter until soft, about 5 minutes. Remove from heat, add corn, parsley, salt and pepper. Turn into a 2-quart casserole.

Beat eggs, milk and cheese together and pour over the vegetables. Bake in a 350 degree preheated oven for 50 minutes or until custard is firm. Serves 4 as a luncheon entree.

# Corn and Spinach Pudding

1 package chopped spinach, cooked and squeezed dry

3 cups cooked corn kernels (6 ears)

1 tablespoon butter

1 onion chopped

$^2/_3$ cup boiled ham, chopped

2 eggs

$^3/_4$ cup milk

salt and pepper to taste

Place spinach and corn in a bowl, set aside. Melt butter in skillet and sauté onion, add ham and sauté for 5 minutes more and combine with spinach and corn. Mix well, then turn the mixture into a 2-quart casserole or soufflé dish.

Beat milk and eggs together, season with salt and pepper and pour over vegetable mixture. Bake 50 to 60 minutes or until puffy.

# Corn and Tomato Casserole

6 ears of fresh corn

1 medium onion, chopped

1 medium green pepper, chopped

2 tablespoons unsalted butter or margarine

4 medium tomatoes, sliced

1 teaspoon salt (or less)

$1/2$ teaspoon pepper

1 cup soft breadcrumbs

2 tablespoons melted butter

Cut corn kernels from cob with sharp knife (not too close to the cob). Combine corn, onion and green pepper. Sauté in 2 tablespoons of butter for five minutes. Spoon half the corn mixture into a 2-quart casserole, top with half the tomatoes. Sprinkle half of the salt and pepper. Repeat the layers. Combine breadcrumbs with 2 tablespoons of melted butter and sprinkle evenly over casserole. Bake at 375 degrees for 30 minutes.

# 6
# *The Potato Eaters*

For years the story was told that Sir Francis Drake, the predatory privateer honored by the British Crown, scoured the Atlantic looking for ships carrying gold and silver. When the rich cargo of a Spanish ship slipped by him he returned without the expected loot and stopped at an Irish port to unload potatoes taken as provisions for his crew. Other stories credit Sir Walter Raleigh, but whoever brought potatoes to Ireland performed a valiant act because it saved millions of Irish men, women and children from starvation. Fifteenth century religious wars had created an impasse that resulted in restrictions on grain imports coming from England and the European mainland. Reeling from famine, Ireland was eager to embrace a new food that could flourish on Ireland's boggy soil.

Millions more were saved by the humble potato during the years when basic European sustenance depended on domesticated grains and grasses, and famine and plague were frequent specters.

A short growing season in Northern Europe caused periodic crop failures which were followed by terrible times of famine and disease. Rye and oats were better able to survive the elements than wheat, but these grasses do not contain gluten, the leavening constituent of wheat, and they could not sustain a food economy based on bread.

Despite years of war, famine and misery, Europe was poised for change and industrial expansion, but needed an adequate food supply to fuel a new era. The Europeans did not turn to the potato for sustenance. It was disdained as food suitable only for naked savages, and the ugly tuber was rumored to cause leprosy. The potato is a member of the family that includes deadly nightshade, so there was some reason for caution. Wheat-growing countries like Spain, Italy and France had seen a few potatoes planted in garden plots around monasteries as a novelty, mainly for cattle feed, but it was not used not as a food staple.

By 1570 food shortages were so severe that government officials, fearing riots and revolt, searched for new food resources. Both Frederick the Great of Germany and Catherine of Russia urged peasants to plant potatoes. News of the potato's success in Ireland encouraged monarchs to consider the potato an adequate source of starch for the common people. German and Russian laws were passed that forced peasants to plant the crop, but food habits are hard to change and hungry people still resisted the potato.

The king of France finally decided on a strategy for making potatoes acceptable. Wearing a potato flower in his coat lapel, with his wife, Marie Antoinette, wearing a necklace of potato flowers, he arranged for an elaborate meal at court. With great fanfare and public display, the king and queen ate and seemingly relished boiled potatoes. The courtiers reluctantly followed his lead. People waited anxiously to see what would happen, and when nothing untoward developed for the king, the queen or his courtiers, people began to embrace the potato.

In Russia, Poland, Germany, Scandinavia and the Benelux countries it became the food staple and replaced scarce wheat products. The potato took on a national identity, complete with a suitable name, for each country's cuisine. The Spanish, Portuguese and Italian names remain similar to the Native American's *batata.* The Germans and Danes call it *kartoffel*, the Dutch call it *aardappel*, in Norway it is *potet*, and in Sweden it is called *potatis*. The Serb-Croats call it *krompir* and the French have *pomme de terre.* The Russian diminutive plural for potatoes is an affectionate *kartoshki*, and vodka (which is the Russian diminutive for water, *voda*) is distilled from the cheapest source of available starch which is often the potato (especially in Poland).

Many countries stake a claim to the potato, and ethnic recipes reflect the character and taste of people around the world. Few remember that the plant is a gift from America. Van Gogh in his famous painting "The Potato Eaters" captured the earthy goodness of the tuber and the honest faces of the workers. Those European faces are different from those of the farmers who labored on the peaks of Andes Mountains 4000 years ago to domesticate the potato. The people who followed them, notably the Incas, built terraces, digging by hand, inserting ditches for drainage and creating a huge laboratory for domesticating, cultivating and breeding a most admirable food, one that ultimately prospered in every soil and climate.

Many towns in Europe have heroes who are remembered for their fight against starvation, heroes who brought the lowly potato to those who had no other source of food. Often they are honored with statues, such as the one shown above commemorating the introduction of the potato to Pilgramsreuth by Hans Rogler in 1647.

The common potato, *Solanum tuberosum*, is not a root crop; it is the swollen tip of an underground stem, a tuber that stores starch in order to support the leafy plant above the soil. If the plant remained undisturbed it would eventually bear a small green fruit, similar to an unripe tomato, but the fruit as well as the eye and seed contain solanin, a toxin which make them inedible. Green patches on potatoes usually contain some solanin and indicate that the potato has been exposed to direct sunlight. The green patch should be removed, or, better still, the potato should be discarded. The solanin is eliminated in cooking, but it may nevertheless give the potato a bitter taste.

As a source of starch and general nutrition the potato is unparalleled and has many advantages over grains. It is easily propagated, as each eye produces an entire plant. It is easy to sow; it requires few tools and thrives in climates and fields unsuited to grain production. When harvested it is ready to eat and needs no threshing, winnowing, chaffing or grinding. The plant yields more energy per acre than any of the cereal grasses. It is rich in carbohydrates and protein, and it is an excellent source of potassium and vitamin C. An added attraction is that when the tax collector comes in the fall to take the tithe or assessment out of the grain bins, the potato may still be safely buried in the ground!

The potato is a major food grown in 80 countries. About 35 billion pounds of potatoes are grown each year in the United States. This enormous food resource is big business, but in its place of origin it is still "small potatoes", small crops grown in small plots by the people who are rich in tradition but very poor in the world's goods.

On the road to Ecuadorian and Peruvian fairs in Otavalo, Ambato, Riobama and other Andean markets one sees barefoot Indians, wearing the style of hats assigned to them by the Spanish conquistadores, carrying small sacks of potatoes. These descendants of proud Andean farmers trudge over miles of mountain roads to bring to market potatoes in shades of white, golden yellow, blue, purple and red. They grow their varied crops on tiny plots of land at altitudes where corn and beans would not prosper. They find a place on the fairground near the women who sell hats known as "Panamas" woven from the cut leaves of the pandanus tree. The man who prescribes ancient herbal medicines has his display near the woman who concocts love potions. The potato-growers are their friends, and they chatter in Quechua, their ancient language, while they spread their potatoes, one by one onto the dusty ground. They sort them according to color, shape and texture. The seeds for these varieties have passed from generation to generation and the potato farmers know their qualities, which were identified long ago by their Andean forefathers, notably the Incas.

The Inca Empire at the height of its power covered more than 2000 miles of rugged desert coast and mountainous terrain. In that inhospitable environment a huge population survived, prospered, and built an advanced civilization. Corn was their most essential crop and some varieties of corn survived at altitudes of up to 8000 feet. At still higher altitudes, on man-made terraces encircling the mountains, they grew potatoes, the plots approaching the top of the Andean peaks.

The potato growers watched the plants grow and identified their specific traits to see how they adapted to altitude, soil conditions, cold, and hours of sunshine. They cross-bred them to improve the stock and then planted the most productive cultivars in climates and soils best suited to their attributes. They learned how to store them and in icy regions they learned how to freeze-dry them to provide adequate food for the coldest months. Freshly harvested mature potatoes, with tougher textures, were trampled by hundreds of feet until all the moisture had been extracted and the pulp was completely dry. The dried pulp was stored in icy caves and reconstituted with melted snow during the winter to provide year-round nourishment. Diversity had more than esthetic appeal, it was essential to obtaining the finest crops.

In Peru the computers of El Centro Internacional de las Papas (CIP), a seed bank, contain a vast amount of data on hundreds of different potato cultivars. They preserve a reservoir of genetic plant material and keep a record of which varieties are susceptible to specific crop pests and which are most resistant to a variety of blights and diseases.

In the United States we concentrate on crops that are most advantageous economically. Since more than 60% of the potato harvest goes into preprocessed potato chips and fries, the bland varieties best suited for such processing are given the greatest acreage. Varieties not in demand may be lost forever, but the danger in a monoculture, where there is little diversity, is that we may be losing a race that would be resistant to a new disease infestation. Should a widespread potato blight develop we may have to turn to the seed bank in Peru to look for resistant varieties. But seed banks are not totally reassuring. Acts of terror, natural disasters and technological failures may disrupt computerized collections. In Russia, a slashed budget now endangers the precious contents of the Vavilov Institute, in St. Petersburg. The Vavilov library stores the cultivated and wild seeds of potatoes, grains, corn, beans, fodder, fruits and vegetables collected on five continents. This is an international treasure house. The Andean farmers on their small plots have kept a heritage of precious seed that are a world treasure, but they too may fall prey to advancing industrialization and the last vestiges of once-great civilizations will vanish.

The American colonists considered the potato an oddity. In the New World they retained many of their Old World prejudices and by 1719 the potato was just beginning to become a market staple. Then in the 19th century the Irish came fleeing from their famine-ridden land. The new immigrants relished potatoes and grew them in disease-free American soil. The "Irish" potato became a major New England food crop, and the entire area was markedly changed by the new demography and the vastly enlarged food resource.

The story of the Irish potato famine is dramatic and revealing. Harsh restrictions imposed by the British Crown during the religious upheavals of the 15th century left the Irish people on the edge of starvation. Ireland's boggy soil produced little grain, and when the potato arrived in Ireland in mid 16th century, it was welcomed and became an immediate success. On a modest plot of land an Irish farmer could construct a "lazybed", ridged so that it prevented soil erosion. In a "lazybed" the crop could over-winter and provide food for a family for an entire year. By 1650 potatoes had become the staple food of Ireland. Ample nutrition fueled an unprecedented population explosion. The birth rate increased, infant mortality dropped, life spans lengthened. In less than a century the Irish population grew by 600%. But the land could no longer support so many people. Potato crops became vulnerable to a series of plant diseases which should have been warnings of impending disaster, but little was known or understood about the need for biodiversity or other aspects of plant physiology. Then came the blight and the famine of 1845-50 which killed a million people. More than a million more fled the country. It changed the demographic complexion of Ireland and changed the demographics and politics of the United States.

The introduction of the potato into Eastern and Central Europe also changed the character and demographics of that part of the world. Suleiman the Magnificent had become Sultan in 1520 when the Ottoman Empire had already embarked on an aggressive assault on neighboring states. Under Suleiman the empire expanded into Africa, Asia Minor and Eastern Europe. Barbarossa, the relentless commander of the Turkish navy, ravaged ships along the northern coast of Africa, penetrated east to the Persian Gulf, and surged into the heart of Europe. The eastern Mediterranean became a Turkish sea, and the Turks patrolled the ports where the main trade in foods took place. Cattle and grains crossed the Atlantic to feed Spanish and Portuguese explorers. Return trips carried New World foods such as corn, beans and potatoes to Mediterranean ports. Many of these ships fell into the hands of the wheat-eating Turks who disdained the foods from the Americas. The ships sailed up the Danube with these stores of American foods and the Turks gave them to their starving subject peoples. Loot from Spanish and Portuguese ships was eagerly welcomed and given their ethnic identity.

In modern-day Turkey, the Turks who originally scorned the potato now make it part of their daily diet. Stews rest on nests of mashed potatoes. Carrots, spinach and eggplant are puréed and combined with mashed potatoes. The purées are spread on ridged platters or plates to hold the gravies and sauces that are the perfect foil for the vegetables. Cubed, cold potatoes are combined with cucumbers and tomatoes to make delightful salads that characterize fresh Turkish flavor.

# Carrot and Potato Purée

4 to 6 large carrots

1 pound of russet potatoes

$^1/_2$ cup sliced onions

Salt and pepper to taste

2 tablespoons butter

$^1/_2$ cup warm milk

2 tablespoons finely
    chopped chives or
    cilantro

Trim and scrape carrots and cut into 1-inch pieces. Peel potatoes and cut them into 2-inch cubes. Place carrots, potato cubes and onion in saucepan and cover with cold water. Salt to taste. Bring to a boil and simmer for 20 minutes or until tender. Do not overcook.

Drain vegetables and mash by hand or put through food mill or potato ricer. Return to clean saucepan. Add butter, sprinkle with pepper and blend well with wooden spatula. Place over low heat and add warm milk. Beat with wooden spoon, then add chives or cilantro. Beat again. Spread onto warm plates, making a rim to hold stew meat and gravy. Serve immediately. Serves 6.

\* \* \*

Potatoes became such an important and integral part of the European scene that it was impossible for Europeans to believe that they had ever existed without them.

As a young lad my father worked in a sawmill in Russia. In winter, when there were no fresh greens, he and the rest of the crew survived on a salad of cubed boiled potatoes, beets, parsnips, turnips, carrots and celery root marinated in oil and vinegar. Black radishes, herring and coarse black bread when available made it a banquet. He described such feasts with nostalgic sighs and shook his head in disbelief when told that potatoes were first cultivated by American Indians. He would argue "Potatoes are typically Russian, even vodka, the country's national tipple, is made from potatoes."

Many Jews believe that the potato originated as part of their ancient heritage. Hannukah, the holiday that celebrates the victory of Judas Maccabeus and the freedom fighters who triumphed over the Greeks and Syrians in 165 B.C., is celebrated with a meal that has potato pancakes as a focal point of the ritual meal. The Maccabeans had never even dreamed of potatoes; the meal commemorates the single cruse of oil which was sufficient to light the encampment for just one night. The oil continued to burn for eight nights, and the branched menorah associated with the holiday allows for a new candle to be lit for each of eight nights. It is the oil, not the potato that is honored, but it would be hard to prevail on dedicated pancake eaters that potatoes were unknown to the Maccabeans.

As a young girl I shredded the potatoes for the latkes and ate the pancakes with scraped knuckles. Now that potatoes can be shredded in a food processor they are one of my favorite foods. Blenders do not work as well as food processors because they turn potatoes into a purée rather than into the shreds that give the latke substance.

# *Potato Latkes*

4 potatoes, peeled

1 small onion, peeled

1 egg

2 tablespoons all-purpose
   flour

Salt and freshly ground
   pepper to taste

Place shredding disk in food processor, shred potatoes together with onion. Remove shredding disk and replace with metal blade. Add eggs, flour and seasoning, process until ingredients are blended.

Remove mixture to bowl. Heat oil in a large frying pan, until hot but not smoking, drop tablespoonfuls of batter into pan, press down to flatten cakes, and fry on both sides until crispy and brown. Serve at once. Latkes are traditionally eaten with sour cream, but they are also very good with apple sauce. Makes 4 portions.

Saving time and fuel is important to poor people. Peasants and factory workers boiled large quantities of potatoes, sufficient for a meal, and enough for plenty of leftovers. Pre-cooked potatoes are versatile. They can be fried, scalloped, creamed, and combined with vegetables in stir-fried dishes. The Chinese and Japanese, who were short of fuel, prepared food over small, fast-burning fires. Green vegetables stayed crisp and chewy; potatoes needed more time to become tender unless they were very thinly sliced. A half-minute head start in a stir-fry will make them soft, but partially cooked potatoes have more substance and add texture when cubed or thickly sliced. (Unpeeled cooked potatoes should be lightly brushed with fat or oil to prevent rapid evaporation and wrinkling.)

## *Basic Stir Fry*

In a fry-pan or wok, heat 1 tablespoon of oil until hot, but not smoking. Peanut oil may be heated to 375 degrees, canola oil or other salad oils are safer at 350 degrees. Sauté a thinly sliced onion until soft, add peeled, sliced or cubed potatoes, turn and stir for about 30 seconds. Add sugar peas, snow peas, cauliflower, broccoli, sprinkle with salt and paprika, and stir for three minutes until vegetables are heated through but still crisp. To this basic recipe add leftover bits of meat or chicken for an elegant meal. Fresh chives, parsley or grated carrots add vitamins as well as pleasing flavor.

* * *

Pre-cooked or partially cooked potatoes have become adapted to many styles that are often associated with distinct ethnic origin.

# Herbed Scalloped Potatoes
## Typically Scandinavian

2 pounds unpeeled new
    potatoes

2 tablespoons butter

2 tablespoons flour

1 $1/2$ cups chicken stock

$1/2$ teaspoon dried rosemary

$1/2$ teaspoon dried thyme

Freshly ground pepper, to
    taste

1 cup plain yogurt

2 tablespoons freshly
    grated Parmesan cheese

Scrub potatoes and cook until fork tender. Remove from heat. Melt butter in small saucepan, stir in flour. Cook for 2 minutes. Remove from heat and stir in stock, rosemary, thyme and pepper. Return to heat and continue cooking until mixture thickens. Remove from heat and stir in yogurt.

Halve or slice potatoes (use new potatoes unpeeled—the skins contain 20% of their nutritive value). Layer them in a baking dish, pour sauce over potatoes, sprinkle with cheese, and heat in 350 degree oven until cheese melts, about 5 minutes. Serves 6.

# Gnocchi
## Delicious little Italian dumplings

2 pounds mealy potatoes

1 $1/2$ cups flour

Salt and pepper to taste

Parmesan cheese

4 tablespoons butter

Boil unpeeled potatoes until tender. Drain and peel. Mash potatoes with potato masher, fork or ricer. Cool to room temperature.

Gradually add flour to potatoes, mixing with wooden spoon until it makes a dough stiff enough to knead. If more flour is needed add a little at a time. Add salt and roll dough into $3/4$ inch diameter sausage. Slice into 1 $1/2$ inch long pieces.

In a large pot bring salted water to a boil and cook a few pieces of gnocchi at a time (do not crowd). As gnocchi rise to the top, remove them with a slotted spoon and keep warm while the remaining ones cook.

# German Potato Salad

4 medium potatoes

$^1/_2$ cup finely chopped
   celery

$^1/_2$ teaspoon sugar

$^1/_2$ teaspoon salt

$^1/_4$ teaspoon dry mustard

$^1/_2$ cup sour cream

$^1/_3$ cup mayonnaise

$^1/_2$ cup thinly sliced
   cucumbers

Slice potatoes while still warm. Mix celery, sugar, salt and mustard, add mayonnaise, sour cream and cucumbers. Pour and toss just enough to cover potatoes. This salad is best eaten warm. Makes 4 servings.

# Potato Cheese Casserole

4 medium-sized cooked
   potatoes, drained,
   peeled and cubed

1 three-ounce package of
   cream cheese

1 cup low-fat cottage
   cheese

$^1/_4$ cup Cheddar cheese, cut
   into cubes

2 tablespoons butter

$^1/_4$ cup milk

2 teaspoons dried chives

3 sprigs parsley

$^1/_2$ teaspoon freshly ground
   pepper

Whip the cheeses, butter and milk together by hand or in a food processor. Add potatoes and seasoning. Continue processing until the blend is fairly smooth. Spoon mixture into a buttered baking dish. Sprinkle with paprika or chopped parsley. Bake in a 350 degree preheated oven for 30 minutes or until bubbly. Serves 6.

# Potatoes with Green Peppers
## A Hungarian favorite

12 small boiled potatoes, peeled and thickly sliced

4 medium-sized green peppers, seeded, cored and cut into 1-inch pieces

3 tablespoons light vegetable oil

1 1/2 teaspoons paprika

1 teaspoon salt

Heat oil over medium-high heat in large frying pan. To heated oil stir in and blend paprika. Add potatoes and green peppers. Sprinkle with salt. Turn potatoes in the pan for 3 or 4 minutes to coat and brown with paprika-oil, then add 3 tablespoons of water. Cover pan, reduce heat and cook for about 10 minutes or until peppers are tender-crisp.

To combine the potatoes with peas, first brown the potatoes then add peas. To combine with cauliflower or broccoli, add a minced clove of garlic to the oil as it is heating with the paprika to add flavor, but do not let the garlic burn, as it turns bitter when exposed to intense heat.

# Baked sliced potatoes

4 medium-sized russet potatoes

1 cup butter or margarine

Salt, pepper, paprika

If the potatoes are fresh, just clean and slice crosswise. Older potatoes may need to be peeled. Drop slices into cold water to keep from discoloring. Drain and pat dry. Dip slices into melted butter and place in an oven-proof dish in overlapping layers. There should be no more than three layers. Place in a pre-heated 450 degree oven for ten minutes. Reduce heat to 325 degrees and bake for approximately 40 minutes until tender and brown. Serve in the baking dish or turn over onto a platter.

If you are accustomed to dressing your baked potatoes with butter and sour cream you might want to try this low-fat version of a famous delicacy.

## *Low-Fat Crème Fraiche*

$1^1/_2$ cups 2% cottage cheese

$^1/_2$ cup low fat yogurt

$^1/_4$ cup Italian style low-fat ricotta cheese

Blend together and whisk for a few minutes to incorporate as much air as possible. When the mixture is light and fluffy, spoon into small cups or jars. Cover with a kitchen towel to absorb condensation. Let stand in a warm room, or on the low temperature setting of a hot plate or yogurt maker. Any device that sustains a temperature of between 75 and 80 degrees will gradually thicken the mixture and create crème fraiche. Use it on desserts, or fruits, as well as baked potatoes. It has a sweet, nutty flavor.

Try a pesto sauce for tremendous flavor when added to boiled or baked potatoes. If fresh basil leaves are not available try parsley.

## *Low Fat Pesto Sauce*

1 cup chopped basil leaves or flat leaf Italian parsley

1 clove garlic

$^1/_2$ teaspoon salt

$^1/_4$ cup olive oil

$^1/_4$ cup freshly-grated Parmesan cheese

In food processor or blender purée basil or parsley with garlic and salt. Add oil slowly and remove to a bowl. Sprinkle with Parmesan cheese, or freeze the sauce and add cheese when ready to use.

From India comes a recipe that combines potatoes, tomatoes, chilies and paprika—all these ingredients originated with the New World paleo-Indians, as a gift to the world.

# Dumbak

3 large baking potatoes, peeled and cut into $1/8^{th}$ inch slices

4 medium tomatoes, thickly sliced

3 medium onions, thickly sliced

3 whole red chilies (or 2, for milder taste

1 teaspoon ground coriander

$1/2$ teaspoon cumin seeds

6 whole black peppercorns

1 teaspoon paprika

Salt to taste

$1/4$ cup salad oil

In a heavy-bottomed pan, heat oil over medium high heat, then stir–fry the chilies, coriander, cumin seeds and black pepper for about one minute to release their aromatic oils. Arrange potato slices in a layer, sprinkle with paprika and salt, cover with sliced onions and tomatoes, and make another layer of potatoes, onions and tomatoes sprinkled with paprika. This is a very spicy dish if you eat the chilies. For a milder flavor cut down on the chilies. Serves 6.

## How to Buy Potatoes

Potatoes are retailed as Maine, Long Island, California, Idaho, etc., but they do not necessarily come from the designated states. These designations indicate the type of potato rather than the place from which it comes.

In early spring tiny, newly harvested potatoes appear in the markets and are sometimes labeled "baby potatoes." They are a treat with a fresh taste and a fragrance that spells the beginning of a new season. They should be treated with the same tenderness given to freshly-picked corn or peas. Eaten with their tender skins, they contain a healthful bonus because the skin contains 20% of the nutrients. Steamed or roasted with herbs they are fork-tender in about ten minutes. All potatoes should be cooked until just fork-tender to be at their flaky best. Potatoes reach what is called the "gelatinization point" at about 150 degrees, after that they become soggy.

In summer the young potatoes are larger, waxier, and still have a low starch content, with a firm texture and thin skin. They are ideal for salads. Steam them for about 20 minutes or boil them in a cup of water over medium heat in a tightly covered pot. Drain, remove cover, and shake over low heat to evaporate excess water, then place a clean towel over the potatoes and cover loosely with the pot cover. Turn off the heat and let the towel absorb condensation so that the potatoes stay crisp and firm.

Potatoes that stay in the ground longer are starchier and have a mealier texture. The Idahos and Russets are ideal for frying and baking. In a microwave oven these potatoes become tender in just a few minutes, depending on the power of the oven. Baked at 400 degrees in a conventional oven, for about 45 to 60 minutes, potatoes become tender and flaky and the skins are very crisp. They are so good that they need little butter or sour cream to enhance their flavor, and the skins can become the vehicle for an interesting entrée. From a freshly-baked potato scoop the tender contents from the skin, leaving about $1/4$ inch of potato lining. Use the potato contents or reserve them for potato filling. Return the baked skin to the oven and bake at a crisp 500 degrees for about five minutes, then, when cool, fill the cavity with potato, salsa and cheese, or leftover fish or bulgur salad. The possibilities are endless. The skin is like a crust that can be treated like pizza or fajita.

The potato that saved millions of people from starvation played an important role in stimulating technology and industrial growth. This bit of history, reduced to a nutshell, relates to the small mill towns that bordered the rivers and streams that supplied water power for grinding and milling grains. When farmers shifted to planting potatoes, grain harvests were markedly reduced and some of the mills stood idle. Human ingenuity, unlike nature, did allow for a vacuum. Cotton from the New World proved to be superior to the short-fibered plants of the continent and the idle mills found it profitable to turn to the manufacture of cotton cloth. People released from subsistence agriculture and no longer needed on the farm flocked to the cities and became workers in the mills. The invention of the cotton gin and expansion of sheep-herding turned small enterprises and cottage industries into world-wide manufacturing centers that created capital and trade in England, Germany, Austria and Holland.

Wealth generated by industry financed the expansion of ideas and nourished the arts and music on what became a new world stage. It is incredible to think that this renaissance started in the humble potato fields of the Peruvian Andes!

Source: http://www.ferdinando.org.uk/cotton_trades.htm

# 7

# *The Sweet Potato Mystery*

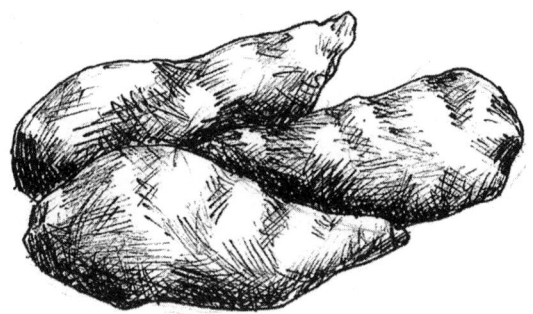

The sweet potato is native to the Andes, but hundreds of years before Columbus stumbled onto the New World the sweet potato was growing in Hawaii, Easter Island, even New Zealand—the only New World plant with such a history. How it arrived in such far-off places is a mystery. Diffusionists like Thor Heyerdahl theorized that Polynesian seamen reached Peru in balsa rafts similar to the Kon-Tiki—this is a raft that Heyerdahl built himself in 1947 to bolster his argument that the Polynesians brought sweet potatoes to the Pacific islands, and he set sail to prove that it could be done. He accomplished his mission, but others argue that the plant evolved simultaneously in these far distant places. Others believe it drifted across the Pacific. The Chinese found the sweet potato in the Philippines when a famine in Fujian province prompted the governor to send an expedition in search of food plants.

In Chinese cuisine sweet potatoes are not ranked as highly as rice. Few sweet potato recipes are found in Chinese cookbooks, perhaps because it is still considered a food for poor people. It may not be Chinese *haute cuisine,* but it is now the most important root crop in China, and because of the huge Chinese population it may be the plant consumed by more people than any other in the entire world. It is sometimes made into a confection or dessert, but it is primarily eaten as a starchy vegetable. It does not have as much protein as white potatoes, but this fast-growing source of carbohydrates is rich in minerals Vitamins A and C and beta carotene. It undoubtedly has saved millions of Chinese people from starvation.

Baked sweet potatoes are Chinese street fare, sold by vendors in many cities. In Beijing the smell of caramelized roasting sweet potatoes permeated the air when I visited the city. The aroma brought back memories of the 1930 depression years when lunch for many people meant staring at the glamorous department store windows on New York City's Fifth Avenue, munching on a sweet potato sticky with sugar. It came from a street cart and was the least expensive lunch you could buy. I was one of the sweet-potato eaters.

Potatoes, sweet potatoes and yams are not related to each other, as was pointed out in chapter 6, the common potato is not even a root. The sweet potato (*Ipomoea batatas*), however, is the swollen root of a member of the morning glory family. Faulty translations from native Indian names may have caused confusion—both plants originated in the Andes, and the names may have been similar, but the sweet potato is the descendant of a wild plant whose remains were found in Peruvian caves and which was domesticated a thousand years before the time of the Incas. There is no other link between the sweet potato and the common "Irish" potato.

Yams are tubers of a plant from the genus *Dioscorea* which is related to grasses and lilies. The term "yam" is often used to describe tropical root crops like the sweet potato and taro, but they are not related. It is an ancient plant that probably evolved in Asia and Africa. Its high starch content makes it an important food resource in New Guinea. Some varieties are considered poisonous, but the island people have learned to remove the toxin. The "yams" in our local markets are a safe, nutritious variety of sweet potatoes traveling under an assumed name. Widespread usage will eventually make yams a legitimate term for the sweet potato—accepted by everyone other than taxonomists.

Our present system of agriculture with rapid transportation, curing and storage make sweet potatoes a year-round crop, but they are normally an autumn vegetable. Look for them in the fall when they are smooth, free of bruises and heavy for their size. Store in a cool, dry place, never in the refrigerator where they develop a hard core and a somewhat disagreeable flavor. They are subject to rapid spoilage and when wet they deteriorate quickly, so scrub them just before using. Bake a medium-sized sweet potato at 350 degrees for about 40 minutes, or microwave for 4 or 5 minutes.

Leftover baked sweet potatoes can make a hearty luncheon dish.

# Scalloped Sweet Potatoes

6 sweet potatoes, boiled or baked

4 tablespoons unsalted butter or margarine

1$^1/_2$ cups grated Cheddar cheese

$^1/_4$ cup low-fat milk

Salt and pepper to taste

Peel and slice the cold potatoes and layer them on the bottom of a baking dish. Dot with butter and sprinkle on half the cheese. Make another layer of potatoes and top with butter and cheese. Pour milk gently into the dish and shake carefully to distribute the milk throughout the pan. Bake in a 400 degree oven for 20 minutes or until the potatoes are heated through and the cheese has made a golden brown crust. Let stand for ten minutes to set.

The sweet potato can be a great snacking food, an everyday vegetable, or it can be elevated to the status of epicurean delight. Little decoration is needed to make sweet-potato recipes eye-catching, mouth-watering conversation pieces. Their nutritive value is enhanced with dishes for the buffet or the holiday table.

## *Apple-Apricot casserole with Sweet Potatoes*

8 medium-sized sweet potatoes, cooked and peeled

4 Granny Smith apples, cored and peeled

$1/2$ pound dried apricots

$1/2$ cup maple syrup or honey

$1/2$ teaspoon nutmeg

3 tablespoons margarine

Cut $1/2$ inch thick slices of sweet potatoes. Slice apples into $1/4$ inch rings. Arrange layers of sweet potato slices, apples, apricots, syrup or honey in a greased 2-quart shallow casserole. Sprinkle with nutmeg, dot with margarine. Cover and bake in a 375 degree oven for about 50 minutes, or until sweet potatoes are tender. Baste with the juices while baking. Serves 10.

## *Sweet Potato Pudding*

4 baked or boiled sweet potatoes

1 cup brown sugar

$1/2$ cup melted butter or margarine

4 egg yolks

2 teaspoons grated lemon rind

1 cup orange juice

4 egg whites

$1/2$ teaspoon cream of tartar

Separate yolks from egg whites into separate bowls. Scoop pulp out of sweet potato shells and put into food processor with metal blade inserted. Combine sugar, butter, lemon rind and orange juice in bowl with egg yolks. With machine running, gradually add liquids through tube. Purée until well blended. Mixture should be light and airy, spoon into a buttered baking or soufflé dish.

Beat egg whites until thickened, add cream of tartar and beat until egg whites peak. Fold egg whites into sweet potato mixture, bake in 350 degree pre-heated oven for 1 hour. Serves 4 to 6.

# Sweet Potato Casserole

4 sweet potatoes

$^1/_2$ cup dark brown sugar

$^1/_2$ cup orange juice

3 tablespoons butter or margarine

2 tablespoons cognac (optional)

Boil unpeeled sweet potatoes for about 20 minutes or until tender but still firm. Drain, cool and peel. Slice lengthwise into slices $^1/_4$ inch thick. Arrange on a buttered, shallow baking dish. In a saucepan combine sugar, butter, orange juice and cognac (or you can substitute some other liquor or 1 teaspoon vanilla extract) and heat to just below boiling point. Pour the liquid over the potatoes and bake 30 minutes in a 375 degree pre-heated oven. Baste occasionally. Serves 4 to 6.

# Sweet Potato Buttermilk Biscuits

2 mashed sweet potatoes – boiled or baked

3 tablespoons butter

1 cup flour

1 teaspoon baking powder

1 teaspoon sugar

3 tablespoons buttermilk

$^1/_2$ teaspoon vanilla extract

Preheat oven to 425 degrees. Put flour, baking powder and sugar into a mixing bowl. Cut in butter until mixture has consistency of coarse crumbs. Add the buttermilk and mashed sweet potatoes. Blend thoroughly and turn out onto a floured board. Knead the dough until smooth. Roll the dough into a sausage about $1^1/_2$ inches wide. Cut into 1//2 inch thick slices and place on a buttered baking sheet. Bake 15 or 20 minutes until lightly browned. Makes about 24 biscuits.

# Sweet Potato Sour Cream Pie

1 nine-inch pie crust, pierce bottom in several places with fork and bake for 10 minutes. Let cool.

2 large sweet potatoes, boiled and finely mashed or puréed

1 cup sour cream

3 eggs, yolks and whites separated

1 cup brown sugar

Grated rind of 1 lemon

$^1/_2$ teaspoon cinnamon

Combine sour cream, sugar, cinnamon and lemon peel in the top of a double boiler and cook over hot, but not boiling, water until sugar has melted. Remove from heat, cool and beat in the egg yolks and sweet potato purée. Mix until all ingredients are blended. Beat egg whites until stiff. Carefully fold into sweet potato mixture. Turn into pie shell and bake for 40 minutes in a 350 degree pre-heated oven. Garnished with whipped cream, this pie is elegant. Without the cream it is less glamorous, but still delicious.

# 8
# *Tomato Treasures*

The tomato, *Lycopersicon lycopersicum*, originated in the Andes as a weed with tiny red fruits growing between maize and beans. It traveled to Mexico and was cultivated by the Aztecs. It was given the Nahautl name *tamatl* which simply means plump fruit. It arrived in Europe in the late 16th century and the Spaniards called it *tamate*. The *tamate* had the misfortune of looking too handsome to be a food and it was simply admired as an ornamental plant. Italian botanists and horticulture experts lovingly cross-bred the yellow *pomodoro* (apple of gold) to increase its size and change its color to brilliant red.

Like the potato, it is a member of the *Solonaceae*, a family that includes deadly nightshade. It was therefore deemed unfit to eat. The leaves are indeed poisonous, but the fruit is loaded with vitamins A and C. The jelly-like substance between the pulp is particularly rich in these vitamins. As we have learned over the years, it is a precious fruit.

However, we no longer call it a fruit, at least in the United States. In 1893, because of differential custom fees, there was a trade dispute about the tomato's classification as fruit or vegetable and the U. S. Supreme Court proclaimed it a vegetable.

In Europe, Italian chefs experimented with the tomato as early as the seventeenth century, first as a condiment and later as a sauce for pasta. The tomato sauces were a welcome addition, they added color, sparkle and tart-sweet flavor to whatever had been bland. As a novelty the tomato became popular in southern Italy, traveled north and eventually revolutionized all of Italian cooking. By the mid-seventeenth century it had become an essential ingredient in Mediterranean cuisine because it is extremely adaptable and blends well with every style of cooking. With meat, chicken, vegetables, as well as pasta, rice and beans it maintains the landmark flavor of its country. In time it became an indispensable topping for pizza.

By 1832 pizzerias in Italy had become jolly places, not to be confused with pizzerias in Little Italy, a district in New York City. The pizzeria was different from the formal knife and fork dining rooms of traditional restaurants and more sedate than rowdy taverns. Families could gather to watch the pizza-makers twist and toss their pizzas high in the air. The hearth ovens made a cheery background. Counters displayed a wide choice of toppings, and customers could design their own favorite combinations. The tomato became a popular choice despite its poisonous reputation.

Raw tomatoes were still eyed with suspicion. Conservative Italians simmered tomato sauces for hours as the surest way to get rid of toxins. Of course the long cooking thickened the sauce and blended the flavors, but safety was also on their minds. Tomatoes, now the third largest crop in the United States, are eaten in a hundred ways, cooked, fried, baked, but also fresh.

A fresh sun-ripened tomato is a heavenly treat that is becoming an endangered species. Mechanical harvesting on a vast scale dictates that the tomatoes must be hard and green when picked. That's essential for machine harvesting and fast transport and handling. As soon as tomatoes show a touch of pink at the blossom end they have reached the mature-green ripening stage and may legally be marketed as vine-ripened. To give them the tomato color they are sprayed with ethylene gas, a natural organic compound that speeds ripening and is extensively used on bananas, peaches and other fruits.

The tomatoes harvested by the ton at the beginning of their ripening stage look good in the market, but they do not have the flavor that develops naturally on the vine. The skins are tough and the pulp is often mealy. If the harvesting machine makes errors and picks tomatoes before the mature-green stage they remain tough, tasteless balls better suited to golf courses than dinner tables. In transit the tomatoes may also be subjected to temperatures below 55 degrees, either because of the outside temperature or because they are transported in refrigerated cars. At 55 degrees the ripening process is halted and these tomatoes never achieve even a semblance of taste. Little wonder that for the home-gardener, the tomato is queen of vegetables, the most important crop of the growing season.

Hot-house tomatoes have more flavor, they spend more time in the ground and are picked when almost fully ripe. They are more expensive and worth the extra cost, but if you buy them be sure they are fresh - look for leaves or stems that can tell you whether they were recently picked or have been in cold storage where the taste vanishes.

Since succulent fresh tomatoes are such a precious crop it is a comfort to know that excellent canned tomatoes are now available. Italian plum tomatoes are vine-ripened, juicy and full of flavor. They are healthful, providing fiber as well as vitamins. Concentrated purées and pastes contain a heaping amount of beta-carotene. Whole or stewed tomatoes are excellent for soups, stews, sauces and a multitude of other dishes. That is good news for any homemaker or gardener who has spent hours in a steamy kitchen peeling and canning the tomato crop.

Nothing beats a fresh, ripe tomato for taste, but there are techniques for intensifying flavor that have been developed by the world's great chefs. Fine restaurants feature entrées and salads embellished with Italian "sun dried tomatoes." Red, ripe tomatoes set out in the Mediterranean sun shrivel, dry and concentrate their tomato taste. They are often packed in fruity olive oil enriched with the flavor of herbs or spices and marketed in jars. World gourmets who can afford these expensive gems savor them.

The Mediterranean climate is ideal for sun-drying tomatoes, but "dried tomatoes" can be achieved in your own kitchen. They are not sun dried but if you want to create a more robust tomato flavor and concentrated taste they make a worthwhile addition.

# *Dried Tomatoes*

6 ripe tomatoes (or whatever quantity you can manage at one time)

1 tablespoon coarse salt

8 fresh basil leaves, shredded into small pieces

8 mint leaves, coarsely shredded

1 teaspoon dried oregano

1 peeled garlic clove, minced

2 tablespoons extra-virgin olive oil

Cut the tomatoes in half, place them cut side up on a tray and sprinkle with salt. Let stand for 30 minutes, then gently squeeze them and pour off the accumulated liquid. Rinse and pat dry. Salting intensifies flavor and crisps the tomatoes. This is a good technique for avoiding watery salads, whether or not you plan to dry the tomatoes. (Save the liquid and use it elsewhere.)

To start the drying process place the rinsed tomatoes on a baking sheet cut side up and bake at the lowest possible oven temperature, probably 200 degrees, for about seven hours. They shed most of their moisture, but are still soft. Save whatever liquid has accumulated and use it in soup or gravy to capture the nutrients.

In a wide-mouthed jar, layer the tomatoes with shredded basil and mint leaves, dried oregano, and minced garlic. Pour enough olive oil over tomatoes to cover—you may need a little more oil than the recipe calls for. Close jar tightly and refrigerate. With this delicious genie in a jar and the help of a food processor you can make memorable sauces in a matter of minutes.

Orange and yellow tomatoes which are advertised as low-acid are actually sweeter because of their sugar content, but there is no appreciable difference in the amount of acid they contain.

For the peak of goodness nothing beats the taste and aroma of really fresh tomatoes. When I cannot pick them from the garden I buy them a little under-ripe and put them in a paper bag with an apple or banana to give off ethylene gas and speed ripening. I don't try to ripen them on a sunny window sill. They overheat and ripen unevenly. Round slicing tomatoes are best for salads and sandwiches. They should be firm and heavy for their size. Never refrigerate them or buy them from the refrigerator case. Temperatures below the 55-degree mark will not only stop the ripening process, the cold will destroy their fragrance and taste. Fully ripe tomatoes, those that are soft and yield to the touch, may be refrigerated in the warmest part of the refrigerator. Better yet, make a speedy sauce or soup to enjoy their ripe flavor.

Busy homemakers rarely have the luxury of simmering tomato sauces for hours. The food processor has revolutionized cooking. It can accomplish in seconds what was once laborious work. A simple version of a fresh-tasting tomato sauce can be prepared in a little more than 30 minutes.

# Quick Tomato Sauce

1 six–ounce can tomato
   paste

2 cans whole or stewed
   tomatoes

1 stalk celery cut into 1–
   inch pieces

1 clove garlic

1 small onion, quartered

1 teaspoon salt

$1/4$ teaspoon hot red pepper
   flakes

Place all the ingredients in food processor and blend thoroughly with steel blade. Adjust the seasoning to taste and pour sauce into a heavy saucepan. Simmer for 30 minutes. In this recipe the salt may be eliminated because the spices give good flavor. Yields about $2^1/_2$ cups.

A more typical Italian version can still benefit from canned tomatoes and the speed of the food processor.

# *Italian Tomato Sauce*

1 medium-sized coarsely chopped onion

2 to 3 cloves garlic

3 sprigs Italian parsley

2 tablespoons olive oil

2 large cans of whole or stewed tomatoes

1 six-ounce can tomato paste

1 teaspoon dried basil, or 5 fresh basil leaves

1 teaspoon salt

1 tablespoon sugar

$1/4$ teaspoon pepper

2 cups water

5 drops Tabasco Sauce

Heat oil and sauté the garlic until golden brown, remove from pan and place onion and parsley in the same pan until onion is lightly browned. Remove garlic, onion and parsley to food processor, and use the metal blade. Gradually add stewed tomatoes and tomato paste to bowl. Chopping this quantity may require dividing it into several batches.

Into a large saucepan place processed tomatoes and add remaining ingredients, put the water in last. Simmer sauce over low heat for about 2 hours, less if the sauce reaches the desired thickness in less time. Stir occasionally. This quantity will yield 3 cups of thick, flavorful sauce to which you may add mushrooms, pimentos, chili or meat.

These sauces are delicious on pasta, but rice also begs for the tomato taste and an especially good risotto may be made with plain or seasoned tomato juice.

## Risotto with Fresh Cheese

1 teaspoon olive oil

1 small onion, minced

1 clove garlic, peeled and
    minced

1 1/2 cups Arborio rice

2 quarts tomato juice cocktail

1/2 teaspoon salt, or to taste

Freshly ground pepper to taste

1/2 pound mozzarella, diced

8 chopped basil leaves, or 1
    teaspoon dried basil

Heat the olive oil in a large saucepan at medium heat. Add onions and garlic, sauté until soft. Add rice and stir. Ladle in 1/2 cup tomato juice and stir. Continue ladling juice as it is absorbed, 1/2 cup each time, stirring constantly until rice is tender but firm, about 25 minutes. Remove from heat, stir in cheese and basil.  Serves 4 to 6.

A mainstay in my freezer is an eggplant-tomato combination ready to embellish pizza, pasta or casseroles, any recipe that calls for a thick tomato sauce. It may also be used as a delicious dip for crudités or as a vegetable side-dish.

## Eggplant-Tomato Sauce

2 tablespoons salad oil

1 clove garlic, peeled and
    lightly mashed

1 chopped onion

1 green pepper, diced

1 medium–sized eggplant,
    coarsely chopped or diced

1 pint of tomato sauce or a 14
    ounce can of tomato purée

1/2 teaspoon salt

1 tablespoon brown sugar

Sauté garlic in oil until lightly browned. Remove garlic. Over medium heat sauté onions and green pepper until soft. Add eggplant, tomato purée, sugar and salt. Cover, reduce heat and simmer for 10 minutes. Check to see whether mixture looks dry. Eggplant loses moisture after harvesting and may need a cup of water to restore liquid. Stir, simmer for another 10 minutes. This sauce will stay fresh in the refrigerator for about five days, or freeze in rigid pint containers.

The French who pride themselves on exquisite sauces rich with butter, wine and heavy cream were in no rush to follow the Italians by introducing the foreign tomato into their cooking. They called the tomato *pomme d'amour* (love apple) and like many other Europeans were convinced that it was an aphrodisiac. But the tomato gradually found its way into French cooking, especially when laced with wine.

# Veal and Mushroom Casserole

3 pounds veal shoulder or rump cut into 1-inch squares

3 tablespoons olive oil

1 cup minced onion

1 teaspoon salt

$1/4$ teaspoon pepper

2 tablespoons flour

1 cup dry white wine

1 cup chicken or veal broth

1 can 14 oz. stewed tomato

$1/2$ teaspoon thyme

4 slices of orange rind

2 cloves mashed garlic

Seasoning to taste

$1/2$ pound fresh button mushrooms

$1/2$ tablespoon cornstarch mixed with a tablespoon water

Dry meat thoroughly and brown in heavy pan over medium heat. Toss meat with flour into oven-proof casserole. Brown onion in the same pan, add wine and broth to browned onions. Boil for one minute. Add to veal then deglaze pan with a little more wine. Stir tomato purée and tomato paste into casserole. Add herbs, orange peel and garlic. Season lightly, bring to a simmer on stove top. Cover and set the casserole into a 350 degree preheated oven for $1^1/2$ hours. When ready to serve, quarter mushrooms and add to veal. Mix cornstarch with water, stir into casserole, return to oven for 15 minutes.

The bite-sized veal is an excellent main dish for a buffet. It arrives at the table warm and succulent. It will serve 12 people with moderate appetites.

\* \* \*

While the French made compromises with the tomato, the English spurned it for centuries. Hannah Glasse in her classic 18th century cookbook *Art of Cookery Made Plain and Easy* gives recipes that mention "love apples" as condiments in fish sauces. Her cookbook recommends that it be used "sparingly." Its reputation as an aphrodisiac may have sounded alarm bells.

British foods, traditionally bland, depended on bottled sauces for flavor. They were often made from fruits like mangoes, gathered from their far-flung empire. Bottled sauces were important not only for the spice they added, they also kept food from rapid spoilage. The vinegar in most recipes supplies the acid needed to retard bacteria.

In the United States ketchup is by far the most widely used condiment. Every fast food establishment serves meals that taste better when doused with ketchup. The introduction of low-salt and low-sugar ketchups boosted its popularity in this diet-obsessed country, so that ketchup still holds a slim lead over salsa. The man who made ketchup a household word, Henry Heinz, got his cues from China and Mexico.

The story starts in China long before the tomato was known in the East. The Chinese flavored their food with a sauce they called *ke-tsiap*. The word may have originated in Malay as a briny soy sauce called *kechap,* which is their word for taste. Sailors brought the sauce to England where it was made from mushrooms, walnuts or cucumbers rather the soybean of China. It may have been the influence of Mexican cooking that inspired Heinz to try tomatoes as one of his 57 varieties. Ketchup's success with fast and junk foods make it too commonplace for *haute cuisine*, but no one will take exception to a homemade tomato ketchup served by the proudest cooks. Start with canned tomatoes, the canning does not mar their flavor.

# Homemade Tomato Ketchup

1 teaspoon salt

10 black peppercorns

$1/2$ teaspoon mustard seeds

$1/4$ teaspoon celery seed

$1/4$ cup sugar

$1/8$ teaspoon cayenne pepper

2 can tomato sauce ($14^1/2$ ounce size)

2 tablespoons minced onion

1 clove of garlic, minced

4 tablespoons light corn syrup

4 tablespoons cider vinegar

Juice of 1 lemon

Combine spices in blender, coffee grinder or mini-food processor until smooth. In a stainless steel or enamel pot combine spices with tomatoes, heat and stir until completely smooth.

Add onion and garlic to tomatoes, simmer uncovered for about 30 minutes until mixture thickens. Remove from heat and add corn syrup, vinegar and lemon juice. Mix thoroughly and strain through a fine mesh strainer. This will make 2 average-size bottles. Cool and keep refrigerated.

Liquids sopped up with bread are peasant fare in wheat-eating countries like Spain and Portugal. The custom of sopping up food goes back to our earliest ancestors and the word soup is related to sop, which gives us a clue to its ancient origin. The arrival of juicy tomatoes ushered in another sopping-up food for peasants, and the bread-tomato combination became inevitable. What emerged is gazpacho, a zesty soup that is almost a liquid vegetable salad eaten with crackers, bread or croutons. Crusty bread is soaked in water and then squeezed into small pieces that thicken the soup. Gazpacho is no longer peasant fare, it is one of the most popular summer treats, served icy cold, with slabs of thick, crusty bread or seasoned croutons. It is served at the best tables with an array of side dishes and crisp greens, but it still has the heartiness of earlier times.

# Gazpacho

6 large ripe tomatoes or 2
  eight-ounce cans of whole
  or stewed tomatoes

3 cloves of garlic

1 medium red onion, cut into
  2-inch pieces

1 cucumber, peeled, seeded
  and cut into 2-inch pieces

1 green pepper, seeded and
  cut into quarters

$^1/_2$ teaspoon chopped
  Jalapeño pepper—or to
  taste

3 tablespoons coarsely
  chopped cilantro or parsley

4 tablespoons olive oil

3 tablespoons fresh lemon
  juice

3 tablespoons red wine
  vinegar

$^3/_4$ cup tomato juice

Salt and freshly ground
  pepper to taste

Combine tomatoes, garlic, onion, cucumber, green pepper and chop by hand or in a food processor. This quantity will require running two or more batches through the processor. Add remaining ingredients. Pour soup into container and refrigerate for several hours before serving. Serves 8 to 10.

Croutons also liven up the traditional Spanish version. Serve the soup with separate bowls of croutons, chopped cucumber, green pepper, and chopped hard-boiled egg to make it a feast.

## Garlic Croutons

1 loaf French or Italian
bread

2 cloves garlic, peeled and
slightly scored to release
flavor

4 tablespoons olive oil

Freshly ground pepper to
taste

Rub the outer crust of the bread with garlic. Cut bread into $1/4$ inch slices. Sprinkle one side with olive oil, grind some pepper over it and broil in a preheated broiler until brown. Turn and brown on the other side.

Garlic has taken on new chic and it is being confirmed as a healthful food. Combined with tomatoes, spices and bread it fits right on the nutritionist's recommended list.

## Garlic Tomatoes

6 ripe fresh tomatoes

$1/2$ cup extra-virgin olive oil

4 cloves minced garlic

3 slices day-old crusty
bread

3 tablespoons chopped
basil

Salt and pepper to taste

Core the tomatoes, cut in half horizontally. Gently squeeze out seeds and juice, and save this vitamin-rich part of the tomatoes for soups and stews. Coarsely chop the tomatoes and set aside. Sauté onions in olive oil until soft but not brown. Add garlic and stir thoroughly. Add the chopped tomatoes and let simmer uncovered for about ten minutes, until the mixture thickens. Stir occasionally.

Soak the bread in water, squeeze out and crumble into tomato mixture. Add basil, salt and pepper. Heat and serve in small bowls. Garnish with basil leaves. Serves 4.

On Mediterranean beaches you can get a tomato sandwich that is a gustatory delight.

## Pan Bagna

1 large round, crusty loaf of bread

3 tablespoons extra-virgin olive oil

2 cloves of garlic, peeled and minced

1 cup of crushed fresh basil leaves

2 tomatoes, thinly sliced (stand tomatoes upright for slicing)

2 cucumbers, thinly sliced

$1/2$ teaspoon salt

2 tablespoons vinegar

Freshly ground pepper to taste

Cut the bread horizontally in half. Sprinkle cut surface with olive oil and spread basil and garlic on each half. Arrange tomato and cucumber slices on bread. Sprinkle salt, pepper and vinegar then join the two halves together. Press down and put under a heavy weight to allow oil and vinegar to penetrate. One loaf of bread makes six wedges and the taste is really remarkable.

An Italian peasant food called panzanella is well suited to modern diets.

# Panzanella

$1/4$ loaf or about 3 ounces of firm coarse-textured bread

2 large, ripe tomatoes

2 cloves minced garlic

4 ribs of celery. cut crosswise into $1/2$ inch slices

1 small red onion, peeled and thinly sliced

1 green sweet pepper, diced

1 red sweet pepper, diced

1 seeded cucumber, diced

12 flat anchovy fillets, cut crosswise into thirds

2 tablespoons drained capers

1 teaspoon dried basil leaves

Salt and pepper to taste

2 tablespoons white or cider vinegar

$1/4$ cup extra-virgin olive oil

Break the bread into 2-inch pieces and soak in cold water for about ten minutes. Cut tomatoes into 1-inch cubes and discard the cores. Put tomatoes into a large salad bowl; add garlic, celery, cucumbers, onion, peppers, anchovies, capers and basil.

Drain bread and squeeze it. Gently crumble moist bread into smaller pieces and add to other ingredients. Sprinkle with salt, pepper, vinegar and oil. Toss well.

Serves 4 to 6.

Leaving the world of hearty peasant food we turn to a condiment that is just right for a grand dinner party. It also makes a spicy-sweet spread for breakfast toast.

## Spiced Tomato Conserve

6 medium or 5 large
   tomatoes, enough to
   make 3 cups chopped

$1/2$ teaspoon lemon rind

$1/4$ cup lemon juice

$1/2$ teaspoon cloves

$1/2$ teaspoon cinnamon

$1/2$ teaspoon nutmeg

$1/4$ teaspoon allspice

1 box powdered pectin
   (Sure Jell)

$4^1/2$ cups sugar

Scald, peel, chop tomatoes and simmer for ten minutes. Add lemon rind, juice and ground spices. Add pectin and stir over high heat until mixture boils hard. At once stir in sugar. Bring back to a full boil and boil hard for 1 minute, stirring constantly. Remove from heat, skim off foam. Let stand for 10 minutes, that helps distribute the fruit. Pour into clean glasses. It will make 5 glass jars.

The home gardener is appalled at the speed with which frost warnings come in the fall. Tomatoes are still on the vine! Those tomatoes that have shown a sign of pink will ripen in the house. Those that are hard little green rocks and have not achieved the ripening stage are not likely to change color. You can fry them or do something better—make mincemeat! Meatless mincemeat has fewer calories and less saturated fat than the old-fashioned version that has bits of beef and pork mixed in with the sweets.

# Green Tomato Mincemeat

3 pounds green tomatoes, about 10 or 12

3 tart apples

1 cup raisins

2 cups brown sugar, firmly packed

1 cup strong coffee

1 teaspoon grated orange peel

1 lemon (grated peel and juice)

$1/4$ cup cider vinegar

$1/2$ teaspoon salt

$1/2$ teaspoon nutmeg

$1/2$ teaspoon allspice

Core and quarter tomatoes and apples. Put through food processor or grinder together with raisins. Combine all ingredients in a heavy kettle and simmer for $1^1/_2$ hours or until mixture has become thick. Stir frequently. Pour into 5 well-cleaned hot pint jars, seal and process in boiling water bath for 25 minutes.

Chutney is another condiment that makes the most of green tomatoes.

# Green Tomato and Apple Chutney

2 pounds green tomatoes, coarsely chopped

2 pounds apples, coarsely chopped

1 pound firmly packed brown sugar

1 pound yellow onions, coarsely chopped

1/2 pound seedless raisins

2 cups cider vinegar

2 medium sized carrots, grated

1 1/2 tablespoons salt

1/2 teaspoon ground mace (optional, but very good)

1/4 teaspoon cayenne pepper

6 black peppercorns

6 whole cloves

2 bay leaves

In a large, heavy kettle, over high heat, mix tomatoes, apples, brown sugar, onions, raisins, vinegar, carrots, salt, mace and cayenne paper. Bring to a boil. Stir frequently to prevent scorching. Tie peppercorns, cloves and bay leaves in a cheesecloth bag and add to the kettle. Reduce heat to moderately low and simmer uncovered for 2 hours or until all the ingredients are soft. Pack in hot sterilized jars, leaving 1/2 inch headroom.

# 9

# *Honoring the Maya with Squashes and Pumpkins*

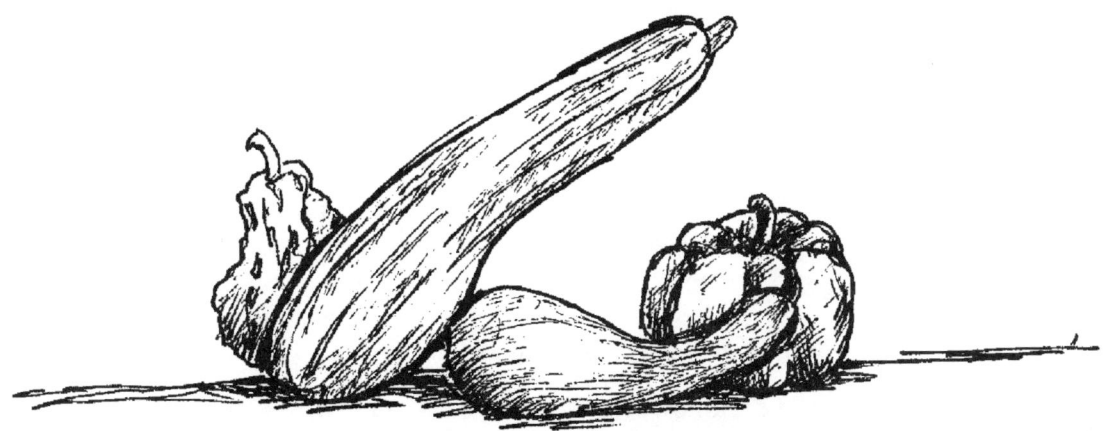

The Puritan work ethic, imported from English farming practices, dictated rigorous standards of labor. The settlers cleared the land, engaged in intensive plowing, and followed a rigid schedule of planting. Their hard work was scantily rewarded. On the other hand the Indians, whom the colonists considered lazy, survived with much less effort. Untroubled by rigid rules, they garnered wild plants, thinned the forest to help spot game, set brush fires to clear the ground, and planted on the previous year's rubble.

In recent years, these farming practices have gained respectability. Smokey Bear now condones controlled burning, selective thinning of forests is rigorously favored over clear-cutting, and many modern farmers, astride tractors, practice no-till agriculture, sowing crops on the rubble of last year's growth.

Thousands of years ago Maya farmers planted corn, beans and squash on mounds they called milpahs, and each year they renewed their planting on the mounds. The milpahs looked littered and in disarray but the plants thrived, and the Maya worshipped the plants as the "three sisters of life"

Two of the sisters, corn and beans, had a special affinity for each other. Cornstalks grew tall and straight, and the beans curled around the stalks with stubborn tendrils. In gratitude, the beans (through their associated bacteria) deposited nitrogen in the soil and helped the nitrogen-hungry corn flourish.

Scientists of our time have confirmed the Maya faith in the life-sustaining qualities of this twosome. Corn and beans together possess complementary amino acids found in grains and legumes and thus make up the complex proteins needed to sustain life.

Squash, the third sister of that plant trinity, was the milpah's stern guardian. The broad squash leaves spread across the ground and kept the soil moist. In addition, the leaves' prickly character kept herbivores at a safe distance.

The summer squashes we now enjoy are picked immature and have solid shells and tender flesh. They contain few calories (they're 95 percent water) and if not buttered or fried are good as diet food and make crisp additions to salads.

Winter squashes pack more nutritional wallop. They are mature, hard-shelled members of the gourd family. Uncut they may be stored for as long as three months (well into the lean winter months), and they deliver a rich array of complex carbohydrates. Their yellow or orange flesh is rich in beta carotene which converts to vitamin A.

Acorn, hubbard, butternut, buttercup, and turban are just a few of the winter squashes that come in a variety of shapes and sizes. The most conspicuous member of the squash clan is the pumpkin. Mountains of pumpkins are stacked at farm stands in the fall and 99 percent of them are carved into Hallowe'en jack-o-lanterns.

The Hallowe'en holiday originated in the seventh century as "All Hallows' Eve" to honor "all known and unknown saints and martyrs." It was a frightening time when the veil between the living and dead was supposedly lifted. We still have ghouls and goblins to give us the shivers and also the "trick or treat" custom which probably harks back to the Gaelic "soul cake" offerings to beneficiaries who vowed to pray for good harvests.

The jack-o-lantern is a strictly American invention since none of these squashes existed in the Old World. After the Hallowe'en celebration, the good cook or homemaker callously slits the lantern's grinning face with a cleaver, then removes the seeds and strings and places the halves, face down, onto a cookie sheet. The pumpkin halves will look soft, deflated and ready to peel if baked in a 350-degree oven for about an hour. The pulp, puréed in a blender or food processor, can be stored in the freezer ready for pies, pumpkin soup, stews and other goodies. Canned pumpkin tastes good and is convenient, but a jack-o-lantern in the yard is a cook's irresistible challenge. Here are recipes adapted from Indian lore and good nutrition.

# Pumpkin Soup

1 large onion, halved and
    sliced

$1/4$ cup butter or margarine

1 teaspoon curry powder

2 cups puréed pumpkin,
    canned or baked

1 teaspoon salt

2 cups light cream

$2^1/2$ cups chicken stock

Sauté onion in melted butter until soft. Add curry powder and sauté for an additional minute. Process pumpkin, curried onions and salt in food processor, just a few turns. Add cream to the purée and transfer to a large saucepan. Add chicken stock and heat slowly. Serve piping hot. Garnish with sour cream and lemon slices.

# Pumpkin Bread

1 cup sugar

$1/2$ cup oil

2 eggs, beaten

1 cup puréed pumpkin

$1/3$ cup water

$1^1/4$ cup white flour

$3/4$ cup whole wheat flour

1 teaspoon baking soda

1 teaspoon salt

$1/4$ teaspoon baking powder

$1/2$ teaspoon allspice

$1/2$ teaspoon cinnamon

$1/2$ teaspoon cloves

$1/2$ teaspoon nutmeg

$1/2$ cup raisins

Stir until all ingredients are blended. Bake in a 350-degree oven for one hour. Test for doneness by inserting a toothpick, which should come out dry.

# Baked Winter Squash Pudding

3 pounds butternut,
    hubbard or acorn squash

1 cup chopped onion,
    lightly sautéed in oil

4 tablespoon olive oil

1 tablespoon chopped
    Italian parsley

1 clove of garlic minced

1 tablespoon shredded
    fresh basil

3 eggs slightly beaten

Salt and pepper to taste

$1/4$ cup breadcrumbs,
    packaged or homemade

Split squash into large chunks and bake in a 350-degree oven until soft. Scoop squash from shell and chop coarsely. In a large kettle or pan, sauté onion until soft, add squash, garlic, parsley, basil, salt, pepper and beaten eggs. Add water, mix well to combine all ingredients.

Pour into a 9 x 13 inch greased baking pan and sprinkle with bread crumbs. Dot with butter. Bake 45 minutes or until pudding is lightly browned.

Yields at least 8 servings.

# Pumpkin Bars
## *An Easy Dessert*

2 cups pumpkin purée or a
    15 ounce can of
    pumpkin

4 eggs

1$^1$/$_2$ cups sugar

1 cup oil

2 cups all-purpose flour

2 teaspoons baking powder

2 teaspoons cinnamon

1 teaspoon salt

Beat eggs by hand and add to other ingredients in mixing bowl or food processor until all ingredients are absorbed. Pour into a 13 x 9 x 2 inch greased pan and bake for 25 minutes in a 350-degree preheated oven. While cake is still warm cover with frosting and cut into squares.

# Cream Cheese Frosting

3 ounces softened cream
    cheese

$^1$/$_2$ cup butter

Combine the ingredients to make a smooth frosting and cover cake. You can make 30 1-inch squares.

# 10
# *The Clinging Vine*

On the hilled mounds called milpahs, campesinos of the Yucatan Peninsula still carefully train beans to curl onto cornstalks. The stalks that support the beans grow tall and sturdy, fertilized by nitrogen that the beans deposit into the soil. The time-honored partnership of beans and corn dates back to ancient forebears who domesticated and cultivated these plants and built a great Maya civilization. For today's Mexican farmers it is a hallowed custom, and for people throughout the world. Grains and legumes are the traditional foods that have been the fundamental bases of agriculture and ensuing civilization.

In the beginning cavemen and prehistoric hunters inhabited a world teeming with game. Animal protein was usually abundant. Roots, nuts, berries, greens, pods, and vines made for a diverse and healthful diet. As populations increased and people settled into agricultural societies, game in surrounding areas was over-hunted and became scarce. Plants that had only been supplemental to the meat diet took on a more vital role. It was essential for early farmers to expand their experiments with grasses and grains and to learn more about roots and other edible plants. Beans must have been a successful crop from the start. The nitrogen these legumes add to the soil fertilizes and enriches it, whereas other plants deplete it.

Three great world agricultural centers emerged, each of which developed foods based on available plant resources. In China and most of the Far East, rice farming became the outstanding grain crop. The soybean, by nature reluctant to deliver its share of protein, was tamed, pickled and preserved and finally exploited as a lavish provider. Rice and soybeans are still the basis of the Asiatic diet. There are an infinite number of ways in which these foods can be combined, from primitive peasant fare to fashionable glutinous rice delicacies and savory bean sauces for festive occasions,

The Near East, the fabled fertile crescent of history, was a lavish testing ground for wheat, barley, millet, lentils, beans, peas and many other grains and root vegetables. These foods eventually traveled all over Europe and Africa and created an economy based on wheat. Breads, pasta, gruel and products made from ground meal were the mainstay of the diet for well-fed trenchermen and lowly peasants.

The Meso-American civilizations gave birth to corn, a grain like no other. Corn was the goddess, a plant so versatile and bountiful that it could sustain people throughout the year. It was worshipped as the giver of life. Myths and legends spun around its sowing and harvesting. The bean became corn's partner and took on fanciful connotations for the rituals of planting.

Ritual often develops from experience. Early medicine men perhaps decided that beans and corn were meant for each other. We now know this to be true because they complement each other and supply the amino acids needed to manufacture complex proteins. Since no cattle, goats, sheep or horses existed on the land before the arrival of the Spaniards, this agricultural tradition was of the greatest importance in providing adequate protein.

Peas and beans belong in the *Leguminosae* family and were once known as "pulses." They can be classified in two broad categories: those with edible pods and those that are shelled.

Sugar snaps, snow peas, string beans, waxed beans, and cranberry beans are all eaten in the pod. They are picked at an immature stage when pods are crisp and tender and they are eaten as a fresh vegetable. They do not contain the protein of dry beans, but each morsel is loaded with fiber, minerals, vitamin C and beta carotene. They herald the good cheer of summer.

In olden days there was a belief that growing things harbored secret poisons. The conventional wisdom of past centuries prescribed long cooking for these fresh greens. Old cookbooks feature recipes where the vegetables are accompanied by ham hocks, slabs of bacon or other fats, and the combination had to be cooked for an hour or more. Food writers and chefs tried to rescue the attractive green color in fresh vegetables by adding a pinch of bicarbonate of soda. Some cooks tossed a copper coin into the pot to counteract what they viewed as detrimental acids. These were ill-advised remedies: bicarbonate ruins the taste of the vegetable and excessive intake of copper can have toxic effects.

## *Enjoying Edible Pods*

These old recipes are of historical interest, but crisp, tasty vegetables are more nutritious and far more popular these days. Blanching is a quick method of keeping vegetables crisp, and the quick tossing of the greens in rapidly boiling water retains the chlorophyll, which means they come to the table as bright appetizing greens.

Buy beans or peas from loose bins and choose snappy, crisp pods of approximately the same size so that they cook evenly—old, wrinkled or overcooked pods lose nutritive value as well as taste.

Wash the beans, shake off excess water, and remove tips and strings when necessary. Leave sugar snaps and snow peas whole. Fresh string beans not more than $\frac{1}{4}$ inch in diameter taste best when cooked whole, larger beans may be cut to desired size. Immerse the beans in boiling water in a large uncovered pot. Keep the water boiling for approximately two minutes, then drain and rinse in cool water to stop the cooking action. The beans are green, crisp, and perfect for a salad.

Blanching may be done hours in advance, but reheating should wait until you are ready to serve. Toss the blanched beans into a pan with a tablespoon of melted butter or oil, season with salt and pepper, and cover the pan. Let the beans warm thoroughly for three or four minutes until they are tender but still crisp. Flip the pan to evaporate moisture and serve promptly with meat, fish, or as a separate course. One pound of beans will serve three to four people.

The French favor a slender bean called *haricot vert*, an adaptation of the American green bean. For a great salad toss the blanched beans with $\frac{1}{4}$ cup olive oil, a teaspoonful of lemon juice and 3 tablespoons of raspberry or mild rice vinegar. Let stand at room temperature for two hours. Serve it on crisp lettuce as a luncheon entrée or with cold cuts, canned tuna or poached chicken breasts for a light, nourishing meal.

For a particularly fresh and lively version of *haricots verts*, toss the blanched beans into a saucepan with a tablespoon of hot butter over moderately high heat. Add seasoning, a tablespoon of lemon juice, and serve in a vegetable dish. Sprinkle with parsley.

The Italians favor a more robust bean called *Romano*. Its sturdier texture combines well with mushrooms, shallots or sweet peppers.

## Green Pole Beans or Romanos with Mushrooms

1 pound green pole beans
  or Romano beans

2 tablespoons butter or
  margarine

2 tablespoons chopped
  onions

$^1/_2$ pound mushrooms,
  thinly sliced

1 teaspoon parsley or
  cilantro

1 teaspoon chopped dill

Salt and pepper to taste

Blanch the beans (as above) and drain. Melt butter in a skillet, add onion and cook for five minutes until soft, not browned. Add mushrooms and cook for ten minutes more, then add herbs, seasoning and green beans. Heat gently until beans are soft, about three minutes. Serves four.

## Green Beans and Green or Red Peppers

1 pound green beans

1 onion, chopped

1 sweet green or red
  pepper, diced

1 tablespoon chopped
  parsley

3 tablespoons butter

Salt and pepper to taste

Choose slender beans, remove tips. Blanch and drain. Butter an ovenproof dish, arrange a layer of beans, sprinkle with onion, diced pepper and seasoning, dot with butter, and arrange more layers of beans, ending with butter. Cover tightly and bake in 375 degree oven for 40 minutes. Serves four to six.

# Green Bean Casserole

1 1/2 pounds green beans, whole or cut into 1-inch lengths

3 tablespoons butter

1 clove finely minced garlic

1/2 cup chopped onion

1 green sweet pepper, coarsely chopped

2 cups canned stewed tomatoes or tomato sauce

Tabasco sauce or flaked chili pepper to taste (optional)

1 cup grated Cheddar cheese

Blanch beans, drain and rinse and pour into a baking dish. Melt butter and sauté garlic, onion and green pepper until vegetables are soft. Add stewed tomatoes and Tabasco sauce to sautéed vegetables and simmer for five minutes more, then pour the sauce over the beans. Sprinkle cheese on top and bake for 25 minutes until casserole is thoroughly heated and cheese is melted and bubbly. Serves six.

# Green Bean Ring

2 cups green beans, blanched and well-drained

1/2 cup cottage cheese

1 tablespoon grated ricotta cheese

2 eggs, lightly beaten

Salt and pepper to taste

Purée beans and cheese in food processor or blender. Add eggs and seasoning. Stir well to combine. Pour into a buttered pan or ring mold and sprinkle ricotta cheese on top. Bake in a 350 degree pre-heated oven for 40 minutes or until lightly browned and puffy. This recipe is an ideal vehicle for left-over green beans that have been blanched. Serves four.

## Dried Beans

Dried beans have always been considered "a poor man's food." They are always available and inexpensive, and because they are easy to harvest and are slow to spoil, they can be stored and shipped. Beans, baked, canned or cooked, were Depression era foods. They were not considered epicurean fare, but that is changing. Beans have taken on a more glamorous role since the consumption of meat has gone down and starchy foods that are rich in protein are urged on us by the US Food and Drug Administration.

Cooking methods had to be tailored for beans to enjoy this healthful reputation. Fats had to be eliminated—ham bones, slabs of bacon and sow belly had to go. Eliminating saturated fats made beans more digestible, and new cooking methods reduce the nitrate gases. Vegetarian baked beans now come canned in a variety of healthful combinations.

Of the hundreds of varieties of dried beans now in the market, here is just a sampling:

- The Black Bean, the common dried bean, is the popular *frijole negro* of Mexico. It is favored throughout Latin America and is available dried or canned in supermarkets, specialty stores and Hispanic Markets.

- Black-Eyed Peas may have originated in China, but they are so closely identified with southwestern cooking that the recipe for "Hopping John" is considered indigenous southwestern fare.

- Cranberry Beans may be eaten as fresh beans when shucked; they are probably New World beans with thin pods. As fresh beans they have a firm texture and a slightly sweet flavor.

- Lima Beans are named for the capital city of Peru and probably predated other beans on the Andean altoplano or in the Valley of Mexico. The limas were introduced to Africa during the slave trade and became the main legume of that continent. These beans are unique in that they contain a potentially toxic compound, easily removed by boiling. In an uncovered pot, the harmful cyanide gas quickly escapes, but they need to be prepared with care. Two varieties of limas differ botanically. The larger Fordhook beans are starchy and have a meaty flavor. The smaller limas, sometimes called butter beans, are delicate in both taste and texture.

- Peanuts, native to Paraguay and Brazil, are not nuts. They are the seeds of a small leguminous bush. When plants reach the mature stage the flowering stalks elongate downward and reach underground where the fruit develops. Chinese agriculturalists quickly recognized the nitrogen-enriching properties of the plant's roots and many sauces were adapted to the Chinese diet. In Thailand and elsewhere in Southeast Asia they are the base for some of the most interesting sauces in a cuisine known for zesty flavor. Not until World War II did peanuts find acceptance in this country, but they are now an important food resource sold as peanut butter and peanut oil. Peanuts will be discussed in chapter 15.

## Cooking Dried Beans

Presoaking dried beans before cooking usually removes indigestible substances that cause gas and indigestion. The beans should be soaked for at least four hours or overnight. The water in which beans have been soaked is discarded. This is an important step because the discarded water carries away some of the nitrates that produce gas. A shortcut for those who do not plan a day ahead and have no time for long soaking is to bring beans to a boil, cook for two minutes, then remove from heat and let soak for one hour. Discard water and proceed with the recipe.

Standard cooking time for the common American beans (pinto, navy, black, Great Northern and lima), ranges from one to two hours. To keep the skins intact, simmer beans gently in sufficient unsalted water to cover, the usual measurement is three cups of water to one cup of beans. Add more water as cooking liquid boils down. It is important not to add salt or acids like vinegar, lemon juice or tomatoes while cooking. Salt and acids toughen beans and prolong cooking time. While beans are cooking keep the lid tilted to prevent pot from boiling over. Cool the cooked beans in their cooking water so that they do not dry out and have burst skins.

## Beans—Cooked and Baked

A wide range of options is available for working with dry beans in casseroles, salads and fillings. To prepare beans for cooking or baking be sure to soak in a large quantity of water, which is discarded and replaced with sufficient fresh water to cover the volume of beans by at least three inches. Cooked beans will require 1 to 2 hours to become soft and still have a toothsome bite. To bake beans, bring beans to a boil on top of the stove then cover bean pot and place in a 325 degree oven. Bake for 40 minutes to an hour. Test by biting into a bean to see whether it is tender. Keep beans in remaining cooking or baking liquid until ready to use so that the beans stay soft and the skins do not crack or dry out.

# *Frijoles Negros*
### Cooked Black Beans—a Mexican Specialty

1 pound dried black beans

3 tablespoon olive oil

2 cloves garlic

1 green pepper, coarsely
   chopped

1 small onion, coarsely
   chopped

Soak the beans, drain, place in kettle with water to cover 2 to 3 inches. Add remaining ingredients and bring to a boil. Reduce heat and simmer for one hour or until beans are tender. Serve with rice (beans and rice, very nice!).

# Stewed Lamb with White Kidney Beans

1 cup dried kidney beans—
   soaked overnight—
   drained, and then boiled
   until tender

1 pound shoulder or other
   stewing lamb, cut into 1-
   inch pieces

2 tablespoons butter

2 medium onions, chopped
   fine

2 tablespoons tomato paste
   diluted in $1/4$ cup cold
   water

2 tomatoes, cubed

2 green bell peppers, sliced

2 tablespoons paprika

Salt and pepper to taste

Brown lamb and remove from heat. Pour off fat. In same pan sauté onions in butter until soft. Return lamb to the pan with the onions. Stir in tomato paste and tomatoes. Add 2 cups of water, bring to a boil, and let simmer for $1/2$ hour. Add beans, bell peppers, paprika and seasoning, add enough water to cover beans and let simmer for another $1/2$ hour until water is absorbed and beans are surrounded by succulent gravy. Serves 8.

# Southwest Hopping John

2 tablespoons butter or margarine

1 large onion, chopped

1 green pepper, chopped

1 teaspoon ground cumin

2 cloves garlic

2 cups baked black-eyed peas, or 16-ounce package frozen black-eyed peas

2 cups chicken broth

1 cup beer

$3/4$ cup uncooked brown rice

$1/4$ pound reduced fat, low-salt ham, diced. (Another option is smoked turkey which will impart smoky flavor with less fat)

1 minced Jalapeño pepper

$1/4$ teaspoon salt

2 cup stewed tomatoes

In butter or margarine sauté onion, green pepper, cumin and garlic. When vegetables are tender add peas, and stir in remaining ingredients. Bring to a boil, cover, reduce heat and simmer until rice is tender, about 45 minutes. Makes 8 generous servings.

The earliest settlers learned from the Indians how to bake beans by digging a hole in the ground and letting them bake overnight. Old-timers still swear by this method which takes us back about 1000 years in the history of cooking.

## Beanhole Baked Beans

2 cups navy beans

$1/4$ pound salt pork (or $1/4$ pound smoked turkey for a smoky taste without as much fat and calories)

1 onion

$1/2$ teaspoon salt

2 tablespoons molasses

2 tablespoons light brown sugar

$1/2$ cup tomato sauce

Soak the beans overnight, discard liquid and replace with fresh water in a large kettle. Add salt pork or smoked turkey, bring to a boil and simmer for 45 minutes, until beans are barely tender.

Transfer beans to heavy bean pot or Dutch oven, add remaining ingredients. Dig a hole, twice as deep as the pot. Place flat rocks in the bottom of hole and build a charcoal or wood fire on top. Remove coals from hole, set aside. Set pot into the hole, cover and push layer of dirt onto the top, then set coals and hot rocks on top of that. Leave overnight and enjoy. This is party fun, not the most modern cookery method!

Bean soups are popular in every country. They are filling and economical. Usually they are made with ham bone or other fat. This Caribbean version substitutes charred sweet peppers to achieve a smoky taste.

## Black Bean Soup

1 cup dried black beans

1 cup chopped onion

2 sweet peppers—red or green—charred over open flame or in broiler

1 tablespoon butter or margarine

1 clove garlic, minced

2 bay leaves

1 teaspoon salt

$1/4$ teaspoon black pepper

2 tablespoons wine vinegar

Wash beans, soak overnight. Next day discard water in which beans have been soaked. Transfer beans to a large pot and add water to 3 inches above beans. Bring to a boil. Wipe charred peppers dry and dice. Sauté chopped onion, peppers and garlic in butter and add to beans. Add bay leaves and continue to simmer slowly. When beans are tender and liquid has thickened remove bay leaves and add seasoning and vinegar. You can give it a velvety smoothness by putting it through a food mill or food processor. This soup is more like a stew than a soup, especially when served over rice which makes it a good source of protein.

Bean salads are an excellent source of protein, one that can be prepared early and served at room temperature.

# Mediterranean Bean Salad

4 cups cooked, drained red
   kidney beans

1 red onion, minced

1 green sweet pepper, seeded
   and coarsely chopped

3 tablespoons chopped fresh
   parsley

$1/4$ cup olive oil

2 tablespoons lemon juice

Salt and pepper to taste

Combine the ingredients carefully, so as not to mash the beans. Let stand at room temperature for about two hours.

For a meatless entrée well suited to a vegetarian dinner, brown rice and beans make a very nice dish indeed.

# Herbed Rice with Beans

1 tablespoon butter

$1/2$ pound fresh mushrooms
   sliced

2 medium sized onions,
   chopped

2 cloves minced garlic

1 cup long grain brown rice

1 teaspoon dried basil

1 teaspoon dried oregano

2 bay leaves

1 quart chicken broth,
   homemade or canned

2 cups cooked white beans

In a non-stick pan, melt butter and sauté onions, mushrooms and garlic until soft but not brown. Add rice and stir until rice and vegetables are blended. Add chicken broth, bring to a boil, add basil, oregano and bay leaves. Simmer for 40 minutes or until rice is tender. Remove bay leaves, test seasoning and add salt (optional). Combine rice with beans for a hearty entrée.

# 11
# *Amaranth*

Lives of great men all remind us
We can make our lives sublime
And departing, leave behind us
Footprints on the sands of time
*--Henry Wadsworth Longfellow*

These lines seem appropriate when we consider the footprints left by Hernando Cortez when he visited the New World and tried to remake it in the image of the old.

Amaranth has been a symbol of immortality since the time of the ancient Greeks. For the Inca and the Aztecs in Pre-Columbian times it was an important food source and a symbol of the earth's generosity. *Amaranthus hypochondriacus* is a grain amaranth that grows tall and has brilliant red, purple and yellow seed heads. It was worshipped as a gift from the gods and provided a flamboyant display, especially in the *chinampas,* the floating gardens of Mexico. Both the Aztecs and the Incas paid homage to this plant with elaborate harvest celebrations. Amaranth was the first food plant to arrive in the spring.

Cortez came to the city now known as Veracruz in the spring of 1519. He and his men watched an Aztecs ceremony where the amaranth seed was finely chopped, then combined with beeswax and molded into the shape of a human figure. Aztecs, who practiced human sacrifice, added blood to the wafer. The dried wafer was later broken into small pieces and distributed to the worshipers. The Spaniards considered the ceremony a demonic version of the Catholic Eucharist, and Cortez, who was determined to expunge every sign of pre-Columbian religion, halted the ritual, ordered the destruction of all idols and shrines, and commanded that the entire amaranth crop be destroyed. Those who disobeyed these orders were whipped into submission. Grain amaranth was seemingly banished forever.

Quechuan farmers in the Andes secretly planted amaranth in hidden fields, but for hundreds of years the disappearance of *Amaranthus hypochondriacus* remained a mystery. About 25 years ago, John Robinson, a University of Michigan nutritionist, alarmed by the shrinking diversity of the modern diet, embarked on a study of pre-historic foods. He went to Cuzco in Peru, the former capital of the Inca Empire, to study the pre-Columbian diet. Quechuan farmers were reluctant to divulge their secrets, but the persistent researcher found a farmer who took him to a plot where he found amaranth growing eight feet tall, with magnificent seed heads and large, edible leaves. It proved to be one of the most promising food plants in his entire search. He went to major food companies and urged them to promote amaranth, but they were not looking for grains that might compete with their existing products.

Robert Rodale and his father J. I. Rodale were among the few advocates of alternative agriculture, and their Rodale Research Center carried out extensive testing on amaranth. They generated a good deal of public attention and promoted a variety of amaranth products that are now sold mostly in health food markets.

In China, India, Africa and Europe grain amaranth was a traditional food source, used primarily as a supplement to rice. In recent years its production has expanded and it is now used as a protein supplement for infants and children. Popped amaranth is a popular confection in India and has caught on in South America.

In a world where hunger is still a stark reality, grain amaranth is a plant with a huge promise.

# 12
# Chocolate

On his second voyage to the homeland, Columbus brought the cacao bean to Spain. The Spaniards tasted the bitter bean and ignored it.

Later, when Cortez shared a cup of *chocolatl* with the Aztec emperor Montezuma, it was served in golden goblets. Cortez realized that this was a rare delicacy, a drink reserved for the emperor and his court. He took careful note of how the cacao bean was processed and he made notes on how the *chocolatl* drink was prepared. The bitter bean had a bright future.

Montezuma II, the Aztec emperor, was a superstitious man. He dabbled in witchcraft and believed in omens. His gods whispered to him and demanded human blood sacrifices. He believed that human blood was needed to rejuvenate the earth and he was determined to carry out his religious duty. As he expanded his territory, he took prisoners whom he sacrificed in ritual ceremonies. He believed he had established his devotion to the gods, but his sorcerers forecast doom.

When his spies informed him that an army of four-legged monsters with human bodies were approaching from the east he didn't know whether to flee or hide. Cortez rode into Tenochtitlan, the Mexican capital, in November 1519. The emperor was stunned. He had never before seen a horse, he had never seen men clad in armor. He believed these men were sent by the gods. Ancient prophesies had promised that gods would send redemption by way of sea-faring strangers.

Montezuma tried to win favor with the Spanish invaders. He plied Cortez and his men with gifts and gave them much gold, which the Aztecs considered less valuable than the cacao bean. When Montezuma invited Cortez to share his *chocolatl* Cortez reciprocated by seizing Montezuma and holding him hostage.

While the emperor was held prisoner, Marina, a beautiful Indian maiden who had learned Spanish from early conquistadores, traveled with Cortez and acted as his interpreter. She persuaded tribal foes to join the siege against Montezuma and the Aztecs.

The deciding moment was the "noche triste" (night of sorrow) which came on June 30, 1520. The fighting was fierce, with much bloodshed on all sides. The Aztecs, despite their numerical superiority, were no match for the Spanish warriors with their armor, their weapons, and above all their horses. Afterwards Montezuma died in captivity.

While the number of Aztecs and other native people killed in armed conflict was great, the number who succumbed to European diseases was far greater. The common cold, pneumonia, small pox and other diseases to which the invaders had evolved immunity over many generations became the key factors leading to the downfall of these New World kingdoms. As disease rampaged through the population the spirit of the people was undermined by illness which contributed to the ascendancy of the Spanish and other colonial powers.

Cortez conquered Mexico and was able to deliver to his sovereign, Charles V (by that time the Holy Roman emperor) great quantities of gold and silver and many slaves, as well as thousands of indentured people in the land called New Spain. Chocolate was not offered by Cortez as part of the gift, nor were any of the New World foods mentioned in the list of bounty, but *chocolatl* soon became wildly popular among the Spanish populace.

The cacao tree's natural habitat is in the tropical rain forests of South and Central America and the Caribbean islands, territory within 20 degrees of latitude both north and south of the equator. The trees thrive in the rain forest's understory. A three-year-old tree produces clusters of white or pink flowers on the trunk and main branches of the

tree. The flowers are pollinated by a minute fly and produce pods that may contain as many as 50 beans. The pod is lined with a sour-sweet pulp that attracts birds, monkeys and other animals. When birds and animals crack the pods and extract the pulp they disperse the beans and seed new trees.

Thousands of years ago farmers experimented with the scattered beans. They gathered them, cleaned, roasted and hulled them and then covered and let them ferment for a few days. Then the processed beans were ground into a powder for a drink the Maya called ka-ka-wa. The Spaniards transcribed these Maya syllables into their own language as cacao. Some unknown scribe probably transposed the vowels and gave us the name cocoa. The Swedish botanist Linnaeus gave the tree the name *Theobroma cacao* which translates in Greek to "cacao, food of the gods," and for chocolate lovers this is a worthy name.

No horses, oxen or other beasts of burden existed in the New World before the arrival of the Europeans. Shards of Mayan pottery show columns of men marching with heavy sacks of cacao beans strapped onto their backs. Llamas carried some light loads, but only men transported the coca bean—a valuable cargo. The beans were valued for more than the chocolate drink. The nibs of the fermented beans were believed to have magical power as medicine.

The New World people depended on plants for food and they looked to plants for medicines. They developed hundreds of ways to treat sickness, and many modern medicines such as aspirin have been inspired by their remedies. Ethnobotanists still travel to Mexico, South America and tropical islands to find healers who have guarded their medical secrets. Many of these may still be relevant for our time.

In Europe, illness was often attributed to sin and treated with drastic procedures such as bleeding and cupping. People used poultices, plasters and many other panaceas, but the basic pharmacopoeia rested on a theory of four humors: blood, phlegm, black bile and yellow bile. Imbalance of the humors was believed to cause disease, according to a theory first advanced by the great early physician Hippocrates who died in 377 BC. This theory persisted for many centuries, and the noted Greek physician Galen (130-200 A.D.) came up with many additional remedies to restore the balance of these humors. These ideas persisted for another thousand years, and these ancient beliefs formed the basis of medicine in Medieval Europe.

With the arrival of cacao, Spanish accounts of medicinal cures were hailed as almost magical. Chocolate contains two alkaloids, caffeine and theobromine, which may induce a mild stimulating effect. A more likely explanation for the cures is that the cacao drink was mixed with chilies, ginger and other ingredients which have a therapeutic effect. After long sea voyages the cacao beans often deteriorated and lost flavor. To disguise their rancid taste a variety of spices and seasonings were added, and it might well be these rather than the cacao bean itself which provided a cure.

For a long time the Spaniards tried to keep their chocolate drink secret, but word escaped and chocolate became a craze as Europe entered the Baroque 1700s. It had initially been enjoyed by the aristocracy and the clergy, but it soon became popular at bull fights and at the Auto de Fé. For the clerics it presented a problem. Was chocolate a food or a drink? If it was a food, it could not be imbibed during the Lenten fast. At times it was banned by the church, at other times it was incorporated into rituals.

In France the chocolate drinks were first served to the aristocracy in silver carafes called *chocolatières.* The lids allowed the thick chocolate to be stirred into a glittering foam. It remained a favorite drink for the philosophers and revolutionaries who followed. When Napoleon became emperor, chocolate was again an emperor's favorite drink.

In England, despite political chaos, religious bigotry and royal beheadings, the 18th century was a time of world-shaking scientific progress. Sir Isaac Newton's discovery of gravity and exploration of the solar system changed the perception of the world. William Harvey's description of blood circulation changed the world's perception of the human body.

Chocolate arrived in London when scientists, essayists, philosophers, poets and politicians were confronting new and innovative ideas. It was a heady time for intellectual discussion, a time to talk of liberty, democracy, the government's role in human affairs. The Enlightenment had stirred the minds of scholars and the Chocolate House became a meeting place for argumentation. Some of the Chocolate Houses became spawning places for political entities that later emerged as political parties.

Novelists and playwrights wove chocolate into their plots and plays. George Bernard Shaw's 1894 play "Arms and the Man" has a memorable scene where a Swiss soldier confesses that although he carries a revolver he carries no bullets because he prefers chocolates. Museums acquired paintings and watercolors with the popular theme of lovely ladies pouring chocolate in settings made famous by Vermeer and other artists of the time.

Chocolate in the 18th century was still a drink, but it was soon to achieve greater status and importance. In 1828 a Dutch chemist, Coenraad Johannes Van Houten, acquired a patent for a hydraulic press that greatly reduced the amount of cacao fat in the pulverized bean. The hydraulic press separated the defatted powder, which we call cocoa, from the cacao fat, now important to the cosmetic and pharmaceutical industries and known as soothing cocoa butter.

The Van Houten breakthrough opened the way for candy making in Britain. Cocoa powder could be combined with cocoa fat and shaped into coatings for cakes, fruits and candies. The confectionary business exploded, and the pioneers in this industry were Cadbury, Fry and Rountree, all Quakers who maintained a high standard of quality.

Then came chocolate makers who degraded and disgraced the chocolate product by adding adulterants other than cocoa fat. "Junk chocolates" had some cocoa powder in them, but additives like potato starch, oil, lentils, flour, and even red brick dust were used as thickeners. There was public dismay as well as public outrage. The Food and Drug Act and the Adulteration Act of 1872 restrained these practices, at least in the United States.

The Swiss chemist Rudolphe Lindt further refined chocolate texture and added more cocoa butter, making Swiss chocolate richer and more flavorful. The Swiss now dominate the upscale chocolate market and hold the record as the greatest per capita chocolate consumers. White chocolate is all cacao butter, but it deteriorates quickly and in the United States is called "white confectionary coating" because it contains no cocoa solids.

Chocolate in the United States focuses around a rags to riches story about a man named Hershey. Henry Snavely Hershey (1857-1945) was born into a pious Mennonite family in Pennsylvania. At age 15 he was apprenticed to a confectionary store. At 19 he opened his own candy business, with the financial help of his aunt. In 1893 at the World's Colombian Chicago Exposition he saw in operation a chocolate machine. The machine had been manufactured by the same Dutch company that helped Van Houten put his defatting machine on the market. That was the machine that separated cocoa powder from cocoa butter and started the candy business. Hershey bought the new machine when the exhibition closed and he again changed the candy business.

Hershey has been called the Henry Ford of the chocolate business because he mechanized chocolate manufacture. In a few years he had his own town, his own estate, fields for growing sugar in Cuba and pasture land for 8000 cows on his Pennsylvania farm. Everything for growing every kind of chocolate was under his control. He was a benign industrialist and the town of Hershey, Pennsylvania, smells of chocolate and is adorned with Hershey kisses.

To please a friend who is allergic to nuts but loves brownies I designed a recipe that substitutes mincemeat for nuts (see Green Tomato Mincemeat recipe in Chapter 8, page 90), and it has proved popular with all brownie lovers.

# *Mincemeat Brownies*

2 cubes of bitter chocolate (6 ounces)

$^1/_2$ cup unsalted butter or margarine

1 cup sugar

2 eggs, beaten

1 cup green tomato mincemeat (see recipe on p. 90)

1 teaspoon vanilla

$^3/_4$ cup flour sifted

$^1/_2$ teaspoon baking powder

$^1/_4$ teaspoon salt (optional)

$^1/_4$ cup chopped walnuts (optional)

In a double boiler melt chocolate with butter. Let cool completely (important because warm chocolate becomes stringy and hard when combined with eggs).

Save washing-up by using the top of the cooled double boiler as a mixing bowl. Add remaining ingredients. Mix thoroughly and pour into a greased 9-inch brownie pan. The point is to skip the nuts, but you can make the brownies richer with walnuts. Without the nuts the brownies still have excellent texture and flavor.

Chocolate chips have revolutionized cookie-making. Toll House cookies started the trend, and they have branched out into countless variations. Here is my favorite.

## Chocolate Chip Cookies

$^1/_2$ cup butter or margarine

$^1/_2$ cup sugar

1 egg

1 teaspoon vanilla extract

$1^1/_2$ cups flour

$^1/_2$ teaspoon baking soda

$^1/_4$ teaspoon salt

1 6-oz. pkg. semisweet chocolate chips

$^1/_2$ cup chopped pecans

Blend butter and sugar in food processor, add beaten egg and vanilla and gradually add flour, baking soda and salt. Stir in chocolate chips and chopped by hand, or whirl them in quickly in the processor, so that they keep their shape.

Drop dough by heaping teaspoonfuls onto greased baking sheet. Bake at 350 degrees for 10 or 12 minutes. This recipe will give you about 4 dozen cookies and the vanilla extract adds magic to the taste.

# Cocoa Bundt Cake

1³/₄ cups all-purpose flour

1 cup unsweetened cocoa powder

2 teaspoons baking soda

1 teaspoon baking powder

1³/₄ cups sugar (the original recipe calls for 2 cups, but I tested it with less sugar and it was good.)

3 beaten eggs

1 cup buttermilk

1 cup strong coffee, or 2 teaspoons instant coffee crystals dissolved in 1 cup boiling water, cooled to room temperature

¹/₂ cup sweet butter or margarine (softened)

2 teaspoons vanilla

Grease a 12-cup tube pan lightly and dust with cocoa; set aside. Sift flour, cocoa powder, soda and baking powder into a large bowl. Add sugar. In a separate bowl combine eggs, buttermilk, coffee, butter and vanilla. Add liquids to flour/cocoa mixture.

Beat with electric mixer at low speed for 30 seconds or until blended. Beat at medium speed for 2 minutes more. Pour into prepared pan. Bake in 350 °F oven for about 45 minutes. When cake pulls away from the sides of the pan and top springs back when lightly touched, remove from oven. The center of the cake will still be slightly moist. Cool thoroughly before removing from pan.

If you really want a frosting here is a recipe for an elegant glaze.

# Chocolate Glaze

5 ounces dark bittersweet chocolate

6 tablespoons unsalted butter at room temperature

1¹/₂ teaspoons corn syrup

Melt chocolate in top of double boiler over simmering water. When chocolate is completely melted, stir in butter, 1 tablespoon at a time, allowing time for each tablespoon to melt. Add corn syrup and stir briskly. Pour glaze over cooled cake. It is thick and hard to handle if it cools off. Refrigerate to set.

Below is a family favorite, a cake so simple and beautiful that we just call it "the birthday cake." It has real chocolate flavor and the dark icing sets off the birthday candles.

# Chocolate Birthday Cake

$^2/_3$ cup shortening

2 cups sugar

2 eggs

2 teaspoons baking soda

1 cup buttermilk

$2^1/_4$ cups flour

$^1/_4$ cup cocoa

1 teaspoon vanilla

Dash of salt

1 cup of boiling water

Cream together the shortening, sugar and eggs. Sift dry ingredients and add alternately with the buttermilk to the creamed mixture. Add vanilla and lastly a cup of boiling water, which will thin batter to the point where you think you have done something wrong. Don't worry! Bake in two 8-inch layer pans for 30 to 35 minutes in a preheated 350 degree oven. It makes 12 to 18 portions, depending on the generosity of the cake-cutter. The crucial point in chocolate cakes is that they not be too dry. Test cake at 25 minutes. If toothpick inserted in the center comes out dry, even if the center looks somewhat moist, the cake is ready to come out of the oven. It may settle a little, but that is better than having it taste like straw. Let it cool on a wire rack for 10 minutes before removing it from pans.

# Icing

$1^1/_2$ cups of sugar

5 tablespoons cornstarch

Dash of salt

3 squares baking chocolate

3 tablespoons butter

$1^1/_2$ cups boiling water

$^1/_2$ teaspoon vanilla

Combine sugar, cornstarch and salt with chocolate and butter in a saucepan. Add the boiling water and cook, stirring constantly until mixture thickens—it just takes seconds. Spread on cool cake. Decorate with candles.

Too warm to light the oven? Here is a chocolate cookie you can make on the stove top.

## *Chocolate Stove-Top Cookie*

2 cups sugar (1$^1$/$_2$ if you do not like it too sweet)

$^1$/$_4$ cup cocoa

$^1$/$_2$ cup milk

1 stick margarine

1 teaspoon vanilla

Dash of salt (optional)

$^1$/$_2$ cup chunky peanut butter

3 cups quick-cooking oat meal

Combine first 4 ingredients in saucepan and cook until mixture comes to a boil. Remove from heat and cool 1 minute before adding remaining ingredients. Stir well and drop by teaspoon onto waxed paper or a non-stick surface.

# 13
# The Marriage of Vanilla

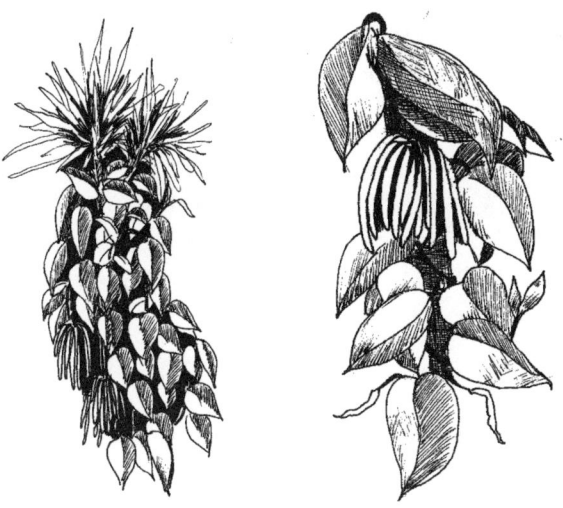

The vanilla orchid, *Vanilla pinafolia,* is a treasured vine, a native plant that originally grew wild in the Caribbean, Central American and Mexican rainforests. The vine would climb until it reached the top of the forest canopy, but as it grew taller it used more energy and produced fewer flowers.

The Totonac people, whose descendants still live on the east coast of Mexico, looped the vines so that they reached no higher than five feet, and the stalks responded by producing more blossoms for the hummingbirds, bees and ants to pollinate. The small greenish flowers bloom for just one day. The flowers not visited by pollinators wilt in the afternoon and drop to the ground by nightfall.

Pollinated blossoms produce pods similar to elongated string beans and they are known as vanilla beans. Neither the flower nor the pod has the distinctive vanilla scent. Only when the pods are fermented and cured do they release the taste and fragrance that we now recognize as the chemical compound vanillin.

The Totonacs were determined to increase vanilla production and they learned how to remove the membrane that separates the male and female parts of the orchid. That membrane prevents self-pollination, and when their technique proved successful and produced more vanilla, the Totonacs said it was "the marriage of vanilla."

Patricia Rain, anthropologist/writer and author of "The Vanilla Cookbook", finds it "remarkable that ancient people discovered a method of cultivation very much like the one we use today."

For more than a thousand years the Totonacs revered the vanilla bean. They savored its flavor in their food and drink. They integrated vanilla into their myths, culture and religion. They found it had medical properties and used it as an insect repellent and potent aphrodisiac.

Little wonder that the Totonacs never forgave the Aztecs, who invaded their land, subjugated the people and forced them to pay tribute with part of the annual vanilla harvest. They chafed under Aztec domination but could not free themselves.

In 1520 Hernan Cortez enlisted Totonac help in his campaign to oust the Aztecs from their land. The Totonacs thought they would escape their oppressors, but Cortez never rewarded their services. He treated them disdainfully and raised their taxes. His followers relished vanilla and probably brought it to Spain. Vanilla was eagerly accepted as an expensive perfume as well as a flavoring, but it was a luxury so rare that it was rationed to kings.

The French were enamored of vanilla. To reduce its cost they arranged to have Mexican vanilla cuttings shipped to Madagascar, Reunion and other French colonies. By 1730 the cuttings were established on several islands, but the vines seldom flowered and few pollinators reached them. When that enterprise failed the Totonacs gained another grip on the world vanilla trade. For more than a century they shrewdly retained a monopoly, demanding high prices for their product, until finally their competitors learned the secret of "the marriage of vanilla". The Totonac monopoly came to an end in 1841 on the island of Reunion when someone learned how to use a thin stylus to remove the membrane preventing self-pollination. "The marriage of vanilla" was revealed - whether this was the result of espionage or an independent discovery, we do not know. Vanilla plantations now flourish in tropical areas throughout the world.

In Mexico wild vanilla vines grow at the edges of pastureland that had formerly been rainforest. Today's Totonacs tend cattle or labor in the fields, while Madagascar is now the leading vanilla-producing country of the world.

When the All-American vanilla orchid embellishes the all-American bromeliad pineapple, the pineapple nut cake should be celebrated on the 4th of July.

## Pineapple Nut Cake

1 $1/2$ cups sugar

1 can (20 oz,) crushed pineapple, not drained

2 cups flour

2 teaspoons baking soda

2 beaten eggs

1 teaspoon vanilla

$1/2$ cup chopped pecans or walnuts

Combine sugar with pineapple. Sift flour with baking soda. Add eggs, pineapple, and vanilla. Mix well, add nuts. Bake for 40 minutes. Cool, turn out of pan and frost.

## Cream Cheese Frosting

1 3–ounce package of cream cheese

$1/4$ cup unsalted butter

2 cups powdered sugar

1 teaspoon vanilla

Put all the ingredients in the bowl of a food processor and pulse for a few seconds to make a smooth frosting. If you are doing the frosting by hand, soften the cheese and butter to make it easier to mix. A sprinkling of chopped pecans or walnuts makes it festive.

# 14
# Cassava

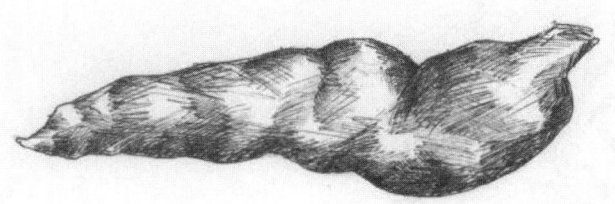

When Columbus returned from his first voyage to America he brought drawings to illustrate the plants he had seen in the New World. He also brought samples of such oddities as pineapple and cassava. Cassava, *Manioc esculenta,* also known in different parts of the world as manioc and yucca, was a challenge to the Europeans. The cassava tuber when taken out of the ground releases a glucoside and an enzyme that react so as to produce poisonous prussic acid. The Europeans wondered how the people of the New World could eat a food that contained such a poison.

The cassava plant originated in the Amazon Basin of tropical Brazil in South America, thousands of years ago. Carbon-dated remnants found on the Venezuela-Columbia border go back to 800 B.C. By that time the indigenous people had learned how to peel, grate, soak, squeeze and toast the shredded root so that it was free of toxins, and the cassava root, high in starch and vitamin C, became a major source of energy.

Cassava is a woody shrub, a perennial that grows in tropical climates and prospers in a wide range of growing conditions. It prefers sandy soils but does well in all types of soils except those that are water-logged. It is very hardy, drought tolerant, and sheds its leaves in dry weather to prevent water loss to the roots. The leaves grow back after a rainfall. The plant does equally well in acidic and alkaline soils and is rich in carbohydrates that can sustain large populations, provided that they also have a source of protein, which cassava contains in only very limited supply.

Cassava tubers are cigar shaped with a brown-pinkish rind and ivory white flesh. They vary in size and may be up to ten inches in length and two inches wide. There are two varieties, bitter and sweet. The bitter is more frequently cultivated and provides a higher yield. The sweet variety contains less poison and the roots are watery, but the cultivar is also grown for its fan-shaped leaves and is used as a cooked vegetable or made into a soup. Tapioca is the only cassava product that is widely consumed outside the tropics. Tapioca is a refined flour which is generally used for puddings or thickening. Cassava in the tropics is now a source of dietary energy for more than 500 million people.

My son John married a young physician and public health consultant who was raised in Africa. Each year she goes to Africa to work on medical relief and public health projects. Here is what she has to say about Cassava in Africa:

"Today the introduction of western food and fast food is bringing changes to the way urban people prepare and eat their traditional foods. However in the villages, things are still done the old way. The Portuguese name for cassava is 'mandioca' (man-dee-ok'ah), probably derived from its scientific name *Manioc esculenta*.

"Manioc tubers at the market are usually used for cooking but they can also be used to make cassava meal 'farinha de mandioca', or a flour called 'fuba' (foo-bah) at home. Fuba is used to make dishes called foufou, fufu, or funje and chikwangue (tshee-kwaan-guah).

"The process of making cassava meal is somewhat complicated, but in many modern kitchens across Africa there is a big bowl with white 'fuba' and a container with cassava meal. Fuba is as thin as wheat flour but fluffier and whiter. The contents of the bowl are used every day and replenished as necessary. Cassava meal is very much appreciated by children who love it mixed with sugar and dried milk when available.

"In traditional African kitchens most of the work is done outdoors. A fire is built inside a small nearby hut to protect the cooking from wind and dust. Fuba is ground in a huge mortar with a pestle and the grinding is the work of women, especially girls and young women. Traveling through Africa it is common for one to see women grinding dried cassava—manioc or bombo as it is called in Portuguese. This is the time for 'girl talk', games and singing. It takes time to make fuba for a meal, so children play and add joy to the occasion. Usually two women grind in the same mortar using two pestles. They work in coordination (one up, one down) and I have never seen an accident occurring from that. Once bombo is finely ground it is sieved by another person, several times until only fine dust remains, ready to make funje.

"Physically speaking, grinding manioc provides a work-out of the upper body, as all the muscles of the arms and torso are involved. Good balance is required as the body tilts backward and forward. Songs and games add a symphony to the task!

## Funje

My African daughter-in-law says the funje recipe is simple: "Water boiling in a deep pan and a funje-stick is all you need—along with a lot of physical energy. No other condiments or seasonings are added. The funje-stick is a tool that you see in all African households. There are two shapes: cylindrical or with a paddled end. It is always longer than 15 inches. The length is related to the way funje is cooked. Remove pot with boiling water from the flame and add fuba all at once. Stir in until thoroughly mixed. Now it needs to be beaten energetically until smooth and this is best achieved if the pan sits on the floor held between one's feet while dough is beaten with the stick over and over against the side and edge of the pan. The proportions are one cup of fuba for two cups of water. Funge is a side dish (or a staple). It always accompanies a stew of greens and fish or meat."

I also have a Portuguese daughter-in-law, also with roots in Africa, who brought me a waxed cassava, which can last for months without spoiling. Frozen cassava (green leaves and sliced tubers) can also be found in some American supermarkets, but I doubt whether this nourishing food will ever become a favorite in the U.S.

I am often reminded that we all have a fondness for the foods that we learned to love in childhood. For those who have a yearning for homemade cassava, here are some clues to safe preparation.

The cassava root is brown and thick and needs to be peeled so that all the skin is entirely removed and only the shiny white surface remains. The roots are cut into squares and the inner veins are removed. During preparation the cassava pieces should be covered with cold water to prevent oxidation. They should be boiled until tender. This preparation rids the cassava of cyanogenic compounds and makes it safe to eat. Cassava should never be eaten raw.

Spanish supermarkets and many health food stores carry frozen cassava, processed, cut and ready to cook. The package may be labeled mandioca (manioc) or yuca (or yucca), depending on the neighborhood. The frozen cassava pieces can be boiled and eaten as potatoes, or eaten with boiled or roasted peanuts as snacks.

The pieces can also be dried on large trays under the sun and roasted on an open fire or charcoal grill, and served as a snack with roasted peanuts.

## *Cassava Leaves*

The young leaf sprouts on the cassava bush are also used as food (older leaves become fibrous and bitter and contain more of the cyanide compound). Put washed fresh leaves in an uncovered pan with water to cover and simmer for about one-half hour. Drain thoroughly and discard water, and chop or grind (you can use a mortar and pestle); put back in pot, cover with water and continue to cook until soft. These chopped leaves are the intermediate product. Today one can buy frozen chopped cassava leaves in supermarkets with specialty food sections. The chopped leaves can now be prepared in two ways and a variety of fish or seafood added. Both the paste and the prepared cassava leaves store well, for long periods in a cool place.

# Kizaka with Palm Oil

2 packages of frozen
   chopped cassava leaves

1 cup of palm oil

1 large onion

1 hot round chili pepper
   (Mexican type), (optional)

2 cans of tuna (in water or
   in oil; drain the oil)

Salt to taste

Thaw the leaves at room temperature or in the microwave. Put the leaves in a big pan, cover with water and boil semi-covered for about an hour. In a frying pan, heat a generous portion of palm oil. Remove from the flame (to prevent sizzling) and add one big chopped onion. Return to flame and allow the onions to golden. Pour palm oil and onions over the cooked leaves, add water to cover and let it simmer half covered to reduce the water, but do not let it dry. (Be careful when pouring oil on the leaves, as it may splatter all over you and the stove. Have the pot cover close to help prevent this.) Stir occasionally. Add salt, chili pepper and canned tuna; if it is canned in water add the tuna water too. Dried small shrimp, or shredded smoked catfish can be substituted for the tuna. Let it cook for another 10 minutes. It is then served over plain white steamed rice or funje. It is deliciously strange! It is a meal in itself.

# Kizaka with Peanut Butter

2 packages of frozen
    chopped cassava
    leaves

1 cup of peanut butter

1 cup of roasted
    peanuts, crushed
    fine

1 hot chili pepper,
    round and yellow
    or reddish (Mexican
    type)

$1/2$ pound of dried
    small shrimp, or
    cooked and peeled
    fresh shrimp

Salt

Prepare the leaves as above. Instead of palm oil, add chopped peanuts and peanut butter diluted in 2 cups of boiling water, and chopped onion. Follow instructions above. Check for seasonings and add shrimp or tuna. Let cook for another 15–20 minutes. Serve the same way, with funje or rice on the side.

# 15
# *That's Peanuts? Wow!*

For most of us in the United States, the peanut that is roasted, salted, and tucked into candy bars, is a commonplace snack, hardly a historic item worthy of a special place in a story of New World plants. In reality it is an uncommon plant with a dramatic story. It is a basic food in tropical and subtropical areas of the world, and peanuts are now considered one of the five most important New World plants to reach Old World kitchens. The peanut has enhanced both the health and economic well-being of people around the world. In some parts of the world peanuts save lives.

The peanut, *Arachis hypogaea,* also known as groundnut, is not a nut at all. It is a member of the legume family, a relative of beans and peas. The shell is the equivalent of a pea or bean pod, and the peanuts themselves are the seeds of a small leguminous bush. The manner in which this bush propagates itself however is unique and extraordinary; after pollination the bush pushes its thin, woody fruit capsules into the ground. Each buried capsule holds three to five seeds that grow into peanuts.

The peanut was first domesticated in pre-Inca times in Peru and was a native plant in Panama, Brazil, Paraguay and other tropical and subtropical areas of South America. For the native peoples it was a common commodity, widely cultivated in fields and gardens. When Spanish and Portuguese conquistadores arrived in South America, they found the peanut an interesting novelty. The Spaniards sent peanuts to their colonies in the Philippines; the Portuguese brought the peanut to Africa and India.

The peanut is rich in protein (typically 30%) and equally rich in oil. In Asia it proved to be more than a nutritional resource, it was a financial bonanza. The plant could thrive in semi-arid or marginal soil and in times of drought it dropped its leaves so that moisture was able to reach its roots. After a rainfall the leaves reappeared spontaneously. The plant fixes nitrogen in the soil which increases fertility so that the Chinese, for example, were able to increase their farming acreage and carry out a program of crop rotation that greatly increased their productivity.

Many countries soon claimed the peanut as their own and it became known as the African nut, Malaysian nut, Chinese nut, kipper nut, earth chestnut, goober pea, etc. It traveled to new regions and became adapted to widely diverse cultures with distinctive cuisines. The Chinese named it *kachang china,* the Chinese Bean.

In African and Caribbean countries where people depend on plants like cassava as the mainstay of their diets, people often face malnutrition because cassava possesses abundant carbohydrates but is poor in protein. Peanuts balance the diet and add thiamin, niacin, and folacin. They are also rich in dietary fiber, and the little peanut is a fine source of energy.

During World War II when meat and dairy products were limited and rationed in the United State, the protein-rich peanut took on great importance both as a solid food and as a source of needed oil. Peanut oil is important in the manufacture of margarine as well as cooking oil and salad oil.

Almost every part of the peanut is used in some way; the kernels are eaten, and the vines are used for cattle fodder. The peanut roots add valuable nutrition to the soil and enhance agriculture. The most significant use in the United States is for the manufacture of peanut butter. The peanut butter sandwich is now the most popular lunch for school children in the US. It seems amazing to us now that at the turn of the 20th century George Washington Carver, an agricultural chemist and educator who enthusiastically promoted peanuts as a popular crop, found 300 different uses for the nut but did not come up with peanut butter!

With all its virtues, the peanut is not for everyone. The nourishing protein that can be a lifesaver for most people can be deadly for those who are allergic to the nut. Genetic engineers are presently working on a gene that will retain the peanut flavor but eliminate the allergenic factor.

Americans consume more than 4 million pounds of peanuts every day. Of this 52%, over 1,000 tons, is consumed as peanut butter. Commercial peanut butter loses some of its nutritive virtues when it is adulterated with artificial sweeteners, color additives and hydrogenated fats, but it is easy to make peanut butter at home in a blender or food processor and keep it natural and nourishing.

Buy $^1/_2$ pound peanuts, roasted and skinned, and grind the nuts to your taste, smooth or chunky. Add 1 tablespoon of peanut oil to make the peanuts blend more readily, and store the mixture at room temperature. If the oil rises to the top, just stir it back in, as this is healthier than using the chemical emulsifiers that commercial peanut butter contains.

In the United States peanut crops are grown on large plantations, but still production does not match that of India, the major peanut producer. China comes second. Many small-scale Asian farmers grow peanuts on small plots or in gardens for home consumption. Peanuts make excellent purées, they add a crunchy texture to salads, and peanut butter dips accompanying satays (a southeast Asian dish of meats and vegetables grilled on a skewer) are considered gourmet cuisine.

Jane Brody, a well-known nutritionist, offers a fairly simple recipe for a popular peanut dip.

## *Indian Peanut Dip*

$1/2$ cup smooth peanut
   butter

$1/4$ cup minced onion

$1/4$ cup lemon juice

1 tablespoon soy sauce

2 teaspoons minced garlic
   (2 large cloves)

1 teaspoon ground
   coriander

$1/4$ cup minced fresh
   parsley

Combine all the ingredients in a food processor until they are well mixed. Serve the dip at room temperature.

In Thailand, India and China the peanut is glorified in complex dishes that accompany pasta, vegetables and meats. The local satays are often served with more elaborate peanut dips.

# Dip Sauce

$1/2$ cup peanut oil

$1/2$ cup raw peanuts

2 fresh jalapeño peppers— or more if you like it hot

1 slice ginger ($1/2$ inch thick)

$1/2$ cup unsweetened coco milk (canned or fresh)

2 teaspoons dark soy sauce

4 teaspoons fish sauce

1 teaspoon sugar

1 tablespoon fresh lime juice

Pinch of salt

$1/2$ cup finely minced coriander leaves and stems

All you have to do is blend the ingredients.

Bruce Cost in his book "Asian Ingredients" recommends such dips and sauces for fresh noodles and vegetables but concedes that they would hearten any entrée.

## *Szechuan Style Peanut Sauce*

2 cups peanut oil

1 heaping cup shelled raw peanuts

$^1/_2$ cup freshly made tea

5 garlic cloves

1 tablespoon coarsely chopped fresh ginger

1 small fresh green chili peppers

1 teaspoon salt

$1^1/_2$ teaspoons sugar

1 tablespoon dark soy sauce

$^1/_4$ cup fresh lemon juice

2 tablespoons sesame oil

1 tablespoon chili oil

Again, all you have to do is blend the ingredients. Yield is about 3 cups.

# 16
# The Avocado, A Vegetable-Fruit

The avocado hangs from the limb of the tree like a Christmas decoration. It is not quite ripe and it is waiting to be cut before it can attain its full flavor. The leaves on the tree possess a hormone that inhibits the production of ethylene, and that's the chemical substance needed to ripen fruit. This seems to be an anomaly in the fruit world, but the plant has other distinctive features.

The avocado is pear shaped with a leathery skin that gives it the name "alligator pear." It is also known as the "vegetable fruit". While ripening the avocado loses some of its sugar content and develops a mild, nutty flavor that blends with meats and vegetable. The hearty flavor and meaty texture give it a reputation as a "vegetable-fruit" and is often treated as a vegetable.

According to remains found by archeologists, the avocado was cultivated in Central America for more than 7000 years. In a land without cows, there naturally was no butter. To the Spaniards who discovered the fruit in the Americas, it became known as "the poor man's butter."

The plant is very nourishing, high in potassium and beta carotene. It derives about two-thirds of its calories from fat. Fortunately the fat is mostly mono-unsaturated—the same type found in olive oil, which is known to lower cholesterol—but those watching their waistline still need to be wary of this delicacy.

California and Florida provide the best growing soil for avocados in the United States. The California variety has a green pebbled skin that turns dark purple as it ripens. Florida avocados are larger and have fewer calories, but their texture is not as creamy. The avocados you see in the market are usually hard, as they are still unripe. Press them gently to see whether your finger leaves a dent, then you can judge whether they have started the ripening process and will be ready to eat in four or five days.

As soon as the avocado stem is cut the fruit ripens rapidly—unless deprived of oxygen as in a tight plastic wrap. Do not let them get cold, as they will not ripen in the refrigerator and the fruit will turn black. The best way to treat an avocado is to buy it unripe and let it ripen at room temperature. When the narrower tip (blossom end) is soft to the touch, it is ready to eat and it should be eaten promptly because its sugar content actually decreases during ripening.

## Guacamole Salad
### Poor Man's Butter

1 large ripe avocado, peeled, pitted and cut into chunks

1 clove garlic, minced

$^1/_2$ onion, cut into chunks

1 teaspoon lemon juice

1 hot chili pepper or 4 drops of Tabasco Sauce

1 small tomato cut in half

Salt optional

If you are using a food processor, mince the garlic first, as it has a way of eluding processor blades. Process all ingredients. Season with salt according to taste and it is ready to use. A thin layer of commercial mayonnaise keeps mixture from darkening.

Purists like M.F.K Fisher protest that the food processor is not the best way to mash avocado, and the mortar and pestle method produces a more interesting texture as bits of the fruit remain chewy. I agree, but such refinements are a luxury. Many dishes would be too time-consuming without the miraculous speed of the food processor.

Guacamole is versatile. It is a delicious spread on sandwiches or in pita pockets. As a dip it is a fine complement to tender young vegetables which should be cut into julienne strips to make the most of both flavor and texture. Guacamole and grapefruit juice make an excellent salad dressing—a change from conventional vinaigrette. Garnish salads with avocado and grapefruit slices. These fruits are pals, they go well together.

The avocado is a perfect container for prawns, crabmeat, ham salad, curried rice and countless other fillings. Topped with crunchy pistachio nuts this shrimp salad gets a new and delicious twist.

## *Shrimp-Avocado Salad with Pistachios*

$1/4$ cup virgin olive oil (or salad oil)

$1/4$ cup white wine vinegar (or a cider vinegar)

2 cloves minced garlic

12 medium-sized shrimps, cooked, shelled, deveined

2 medium-size avocados

2 tablespoons salted pistachios, coarsely chopped.

Cut avocados in half lengthwise, remove pit. With a teaspoon carefully scoop out bite-size pieces, leaving avocado skin intact. Squeeze a little lemon juice onto shells to keep from darkening. Add avocado pieces to shrimp. Toss with oil, vinegar and minced garlic. Prepare several hours in advance and let mixture rest in refrigerator.

To serve, fill the shells and top with chopped pistachios. You need no other garnish, the nuts are decorative. Do not mash the avocado bits when tossing—they add interesting texture.

Pasta salads go well with mashed avocado and balsamic vinegar.

# *Pasta Salad with Avocado dressing*

$^1/_2$ pound *fusili* (corkscrew pasta) or other thick pasta

2 tablespoons chili-flavored oil or extra virgin olive oil

3 scallions, thinly sliced

1 red sweet pepper, coarsely chopped

Medium zucchini, coarsely chopped, lightly salted and allowed to drain for 30 minutes, then dry with paper towel

12 small broccoli florets, blanched until just tender, then cooled in ice water

$^1/_2$ cup chopped fresh basil leaves

2 cloves of garlic, minced

1 medium avocado, peeled and coarsely chopped

2 tablespoons freshly grated Parmesan cheese

1 tablespoon Dijon-style mustard

2 tablespoons Balsamic vinegar or 3 tablespoons 5% cider vinegar

1 tablespoon granulated sugar

Salt and freshly-ground pepper to taste

Cook pasta in boiling water according to directions. Do not overcook. Drain and toss in a large bowl with chili-flavored oil. Cool to room temperature, stirring occasionally to coat pasta thoroughly.

Add scallions, red pepper, zucchini, basil leaves and most of the broccoli florets, reserve a few for garnish.

Whisk together garlic, avocado, cheese, mustard, vinegar, sugar, salt and pepper. When mixture has consistency of mayonnaise, pour over pasta and mix thoroughly.

Allow pasta to sit at room temperature for at least 2 hours before serving, or chill overnight in refrigerator and return to room temperature before serving the next day.

# 17

# Pineapple, the Edible Bromeliad

On his second voyage to the New World, Columbus collected on the island of Guadeloupe a tough perennial plant that became the sensation of the courts of Spain and France. It was called *ananas* or "sugar loaf" because of its marvelous taste. Columbus called pineapple the most delicious fruit in the world.

The pineapple's unique shape intrigued architects, artists and designers. They were inspired to capture the plant's motif and incorporate it into furniture and architectural decorations, coats of arms, ornamental borders, and Renaissance paintings. The pineapple design was placed a top wooden headposts of bedstands and on the backs of chairs.

The plant belongs to a family now known as bromeliads, named after the Swedish botanist Olaf Bromel. The star of the family, and its only edible member, is the pineapple, and it was this delicious fruit that Columbus brought back to plaudits in Spain.

Bromeliads originated in South America after the formation of the Atlantic Ocean some 100 million years ago; more than half the hundreds of species are "air plants." Gradually bromeliads spread by way of the West Indies and the Isthmus of Panama into subtropical parts of the United States.

In Florida these "air plants" grow on the limbs of live oaks, palms and fig trees. Their impressive flower stalks are conspicuous in the spring. The pineapple is one of the terrestrial bromeliads.

Pineapples are now grown in Asia and Africa, and they are Hawaii's major crop. Like melons, they will not ripen when cut unless the ripening process has already begun. A ripe pineapple loses some of its green color, but a more reliable test for ripeness is a solid sound when thumped. Also, the fruit should look large in relation to the leaf crown.

Gelatin packages warn against using fresh pineapple in recipes. The fruit contains the enzyme bromelin that breaks down protein. Since gelatin consists of protein, fresh pineapple will turn it into a soupy mess. When heated, the enzyme is killed, and canned pineapple, which is not effective as a tenderizer, is safe to use in gelatin salads.

Crushed pineapple is a moist, zestful ingredient in many cakes and quick breads. In the refrigerator baked goods made with pineapple can remain fresh-tasting and flavorful for more than a week.

It is hard to improve on the taste of fresh pineapple, but a hearty cookie can capture the taste and provide a nourishing treat.

# Carrot-Pineapple Cookies

2 cups all-purpose flour

1 $1/2$ teaspoons baking powder

1 $1/2$ teaspoons cinnamon

1 $1/2$ teaspoons ground ginger

1 teaspoon ground nutmeg

$1/2$ cup margarine, softened

$1/3$ cup firmly packed brown
    sugar

1 beaten egg

$1/2$ teaspoon vanilla extract

1 cup shredded carrots

1 (8 ounce) can unsweetened
    crushed pineapple, drained

Combine first 5 ingredients, stir well and set aside. Cream the margarine; gradually add sugar, egg and vanilla. Stir in flour mixture and gently stir in carrots and pineapple. Drop dough on cookie sheet in rounded teaspoonfuls, about 2 inches apart. Bake in a preheated 350 degree oven for about 12 minutes or until golden brown. Yields about 5 dozen cookies.

# 18
# Food Fashions

Historians delight in describing the exotic banquets of Imperial Rome and the feasts laid out by the merchants and lords of the Middle Ages. Tables groaned under the weight of large joints of meat, capons, geese, and salted fish. Commoners, on the other hand, had little meat on the table. Meat consumption world-wide is still a luxury reserved for the affluent.

All over the world people depend on rice, wheat, cereal grains, legumes and tubers as the mainstay of their diet. During the 17th and 18th centuries when populations increased in Europe, the Industrial Revolution drove workers to the cities. The poor among them had no more than 10% of their caloric intake in meat. In northern Europe they survived on dark bread, cabbage, beans and greens when these were available. Chinese peasants lived on rice and a bit of pork together with seasonal greens. India became famous for spicy sauces served with rice and vegetables. Maize, ground in the *metate* and flattened into cakes, was the food of Mexicans. Gruel or some form of bread made from grain has been the substance of life for vast numbers of people.

Agricultural techniques have improved and so has animal husbandry, to the extent that our modern supermarkets display incredible abundance in every department. Perishables—dairy, meats, fish—are displayed in refrigerated cases along the periphery of the store. In the center and on the aisles are cereals, grains, baking supplies. These are traditional foodstuffs, staples that have been elevated to higher status now that we understand their role in the diet. Plants are the mainstay of our diet and they constitute

90% of the food we eat. The grains that we do not consume are fed to animals which eventually reach our table.

America is again the wellspring of world sustenance, which makes our problem of obesity an embarrassment as well as a health problem. But world hunger still exists, and the media bring us pictures of starving children which make us flinch and recoil.

Food resources and overeating may not be the entire story, for we may be driven by forces not accessible to reason. Food as a way of life may not be a fashion statement nor need it be a substitute for other lacks. Our evolutionary past informs us that food fuels life, affords pleasure, provides sociability and stimulates brain power. As a species we have been ingenious in creating food and thriving on our ingenuity. But food fashions change, and because I was born in 1908, I know how much our eating habits have changed in the past century. Time-saving technology, scientific advances and knowledge of nutrition have made enormous changes, not merely as a source of sustenance, but as a class statement and a cultural barometer. The rich are now thinner, while it is the poor who find comfort in overeating. But that pattern may change, as has been the case in the past. I am reminded of just a few examples.

David Fairchild, a noted food explorer whose name is celebrated in the world-famous Fairchild Tropical Gardens of Coral Gables, Florida, tells a memorable tale in his book "The World Is My Garden." It is of a 19th century Jewish tribe in Tunisia where all the women were of tremendous size and girth. An informant explained to Fairchild that young girls in that tribe were betrothed in early childhood. A loose bracelet was slipped onto the girl's ankle, and when she grew tall enough and large enough for the flesh in the anklet to be overflowing, the marriage took place. We can assume that the obesity gene ran rampant in that tribe. Skinny girls found no husbands and had no children, so only the obese had progeny. But then the tribe may have died out from cancer, heart ailments and all the other ills associated with obesity.

Another tale, this from a survivor of a concentration camp, is about the evil days early in the Hitler regime. In that lean season thin girls also had no chance of attracting a beau. Well-padded young women seemingly had daddies with enough money to feed the family.

Now it is thin girls who bespeak wealth: diet programs, spas, exercise routines can be expensive. The poor might find comfort in bags of potato chips and fatty fast foods. Food still makes a statement, and the less time we spend in the kitchen, the greater our obsessive preoccupation with snacks.

If you look at the table of contents you will see that the recipes here are largely made up of grains, fruits and vegetables, with modest quantities of meat, fish and dairy products. They require little time for preparation, they are made up of easily accessible ingredients and they constitute the healthiest diet in the world.

Because so many of them stem from the peasant diets of other centuries, they are in general inexpensive and hearty. They delight my taste buds and I hope they will delight yours.

# Bibliography

*Books that Whetted my Appetite for*
*New World Food History*

Anon. 1900. *Vanilla*. Joseph Burnett Company, Boston.

Brody, Jane E. 1985. *Jane Brody's Good Food Book: Living the High-Carbohydrate Way*. W. W. Norton, New York.

Burros, Marian. 1978. *Pure and Simple: Delicious Recipes for Additive-Free Cooking*. William Morrow & Company, New York.

Child, Julia, Louisette Bertholle and Simone Beck. 1961. *Mastering the Art of French Cooking*. Knopf, New York.

Coe, Sophie, and Michael Coe. 1996. *The True History of Chocolate*. Thames and Hudson, New York.

Cost, Bruce. 1988. *Asian Ingredients: A Guide to the Foodstuffs of China, Japan, Korea, Thailand, and Vietnam*. William Morrow, New York.

Davidson, Alan, editor. 1999. *The Oxford Companion to Food*. Oxford University Press, New York.

Edwards, John. 1984. *The Roman Cookery of Apicius*. Rider, London.

Farb, Peter and George Armelagos. 1980. *Consuming Passion: the anthropology of eating*. Washington Square Books, New York.

Farmer, Fannie Merritt. 1896. *The Original Boston Cooking-School Cook Book— 1896. (Facsimile Edition)*. Weathervane Books, New York.

Fernandez-Armesto, Felipe. 2002. *Near a Thousand Tables: A History of Food*. Free Press, New York.

Fisher, M. F. K. 1968. *With Bold Knife and Fork*. Perigee Books, New York.

Foster, Nelson and Linda S. Cordell, editors. 1999. *Chilies to Chocolate—Food the Americas Gave the World*. Univ. of Arizona Press, Tucson.

Fussell, Betty. 1992. *The story of Corn—The myths and history, the culture and agriculture, the art and science of America's quintessential crop*. Alfred A. Knopf, New York.

Gitlitz, David M., and Linda Kay Davidson. 1999. *A Drizzle of Honey: The Lives and Recipes of Spain's Secret Jews*. St. Martin's Press, New York.

Harris, Marvin. 1978. *Cannibals & Kings*. Collins, London.

Hess, John L., and Karen Hess. 1977. *The Taste of America*. Grossman, New York.

Hobhouse, Henry. 1988. *Seeds of Change—Five Plants that Changed the World*. Harper & Row, New York.

Kurlansky, Mark. 1998. *Cod: A Biography of the Fish That Changed the World*. Penguin, New York.

Kurlansky, Mark. 2002. *Salt: A World History*. Walker, New York.

McGee, Harold. 1984. *On Food and Cooking—The Science and Lore of the Kitchen*. Charles Scribner & Son, New York.

Margen, Sheldon. 1992. *The Wellness Encyclopedia of Food and Nutrition: How to Buy, Store, and Prepare Every Variety of Fresh Food*. Rebus, New York.

Morton, Julia F. 1987. *Fruits of Warm Climates*. Miami. Long out of print, but currently available on the web at http://www.hort.purdue.edu/newcrop/morton/index.html.

Nickerson, Jane. 1973. *Jane Nickerson's Florida Cookbook*. Florida University Press, Gainesville.

Pépin, Jacques. 1982. *Everyday Cooking With Jacques Pépin*. Harper & Row, New York.

Reynolds, Doris. 1991. *Let's Talk Food from A to Z*. Enterprise Publishing, Naples, FL.

Rombauer, Irma S., and Marion Rombauer Becker. 1975. *Joy of Cooking*. Bobbs-Merrill, Indianapolis.

Sahni, Julie. 1980. *Classic Indian Cooking*. William Morrow & Company, New York.

Sokolov, Raymond. 1991. *Why We Eat What We Eat*. Summit Books, New York.

Swahn, Jan Ojvind. 1991. *The Lore of Spices: Their History, Nature and Uses Around the World*. AB Nordbok, Gothenburg.

Visser, Margaret. 1991. *The Rituals of Dinner: The Origins, Evolution, Eccentricities, and Meaning of Table Manners*. HarperCollins, Toronto.

Weatherford, Jack. 1988. *Indian Givers—How the Indians of the Americas transformed the World*. Fawcett Columbine, New York.

Weatherford, Jack. 1992. *Native Roots. How the Indians enriched America*. Crown Publishers, New York.

Wolke, Robert L. 2002. *What Einstein Told His Cook—Kitchen Science Explained*. W.W. Norton & Company, New York.

# Appendix

The biological relationships between the different food plants discussed in this book, and their connection to plants found elsewhere in the world, is a fascinating topic by itself. This appendix gives a bit of perspective on how they are all related from the viewpoint of a botanist. The information below follows the *Taxonomy of Vascular Plants* by G.H.M. Lawrence, published in 1951 by Macmillan Co., New York.

Phylum **Angiospermae** — the flowering plants
Class **Monocotyledoneae**, the monocots—a single cotyledon or seed leaf
Order Glumiflorae
    Gramineae, the grass family (approx. 50 genera, worldwide)
     *Zea mays*—maize or corn
Order Farinosae
    Bromeliaceae, the pineapple family (50 genera, tropical to temperate America)
     *Ananas comosus*—pineapple
Order Liliiflorae
  Suborder Liliineae
    Dioscoreaceae, the yam family (10 genera, tropics and subtropics of the world)
     *Dioscorea* spp—600 species mostly from tropical America
      *D. batatas*—a yam of the Far East
Order Microspermae
    Orchidaceae, the orchid family (450 genera, worldwide)
     *Vanilla pinafolia*—vanilla orchid
Class **Dicotyledoneae**, the dicots—two cotyledons or seed leaves
Order Piperales
    Piperaceae, the pepper family (10-12 genera, pantropical)
     *Piper nigram*—unripe fruit = black pepper; ripe fruit = white pepper
Order Centrospernae
    Amaranthaceae, the amaranth family (64 genera, primarily tropical Amer. & Africa)
     *Amaranthus hypochondriacus*—Mexican amaranth
Order Ranales
  Suborder Magnoliineae
    Lauraceae, the laurel family (45 genera, mostly in tropical SE Asia & America)
     *Persea Americana*—avocado
Order Malvales
  Suborder Malvineae
    Sterculiaceae, sterculia family (50 genera, pantropical and pansubtropical)
     *Theobroma cacao*—chocolate tree, tropical America

Order Rosales
  Suborder Rosinae
    Leguminosae, the pea family (550 genera, worldwide)
      *Arachis hypogaea*—peanut or groundnut
      *Glycine* sp.—soybean
      *Lens* sp.—lentils
      *Phaseolus vulgaris*—garden beans (Mexico & Central America)
      *Pisum* sp.—garden peas
Order Geraniales
  Suborder Tricocceae
    Euphorbiaceae, the spurge family (283 genera, worldwide)
      *Manihot* (*Manioc*) *esculenta*—cassava or manioc
Order Tubilorae
  Suborder Convolvulineae
    Convolvulaceae, the morning-glory family
      *Ipomoea batatas*—sweet potato
  Suborder Solanineae
    Solanaceae, the nightshade family (85 genera, tropical and South America)
      *Solanum* spp.—potato and eggplant
        *S. tuberosum*—common potato
      *Lycopersicon*—tomato
      *Capsicum*—red pepper
        *C. frutescens*—chili pepper
        *C. tetragona*—bonnet pepper (paprika)
      [*Nicotiana*—tobacco]
Order Cucurbitales
    Cucurbitaceae, the gourd family (100 genera, pantropical)
      *Cucurbita*—pumpkin and squash

# Acknowledgements

The publication of this book has brought my family together in a way that I had not anticipated. I am accustomed to the old maxim "no man is a hero in his own country" so I was somewhat diffident when I asked members of my family to read my manuscript. Their response has been more than gratifying.

My son Bill Silvert, physicist, oceanographer, computer modeler and science editor, edited the manuscript with the same enthusiasm that he would show his scientific colleagues.

My son John Oppenheimer, who teaches biology and environmental science at the Staten Island campus of the City University of New York, read the manuscript with a critical eye, and his suggestions and amendments added vital substance to the text.

John is married to a young physician and public health consultant who was raised in Africa. Each year Ana Paula goes to Africa to work on medical relief and public health projects. She is a superb organizer and her suggestions for the format and substance of the book proved to be appropriate for the style of the book.

Other members of the family contributed to the final manuscript. Bill's wife Emília Cunha, an oceanographer, read the manuscript and offered helpful comments. My very capable granddaughter Rebecca Silvert, who is a linguist, arrived on the scene when the layout of the book was being designed, and Becka helped make the format interesting and easy to read.

My son Tony Oppenheimer, a physician, prompted me to warn of the allergies that are caused by some foods. His wife Valerie is a demographer and reminds me that ultimately it is food resources that sustain populations.

I thank them all.

# The Author

Vicki Oppenheimer was born in the Bronx, N.Y. in 1908. She went to New York City public schools and attended Hunter College. For many years Vicki worked for a literary agent. She also published articles in major magazines on subjects dealing with travel, child care, the environment and food. World War II was a time of global upheaval, and as an army wife she left New York City and followed her husband, a Flight Surgeon in the US Air Force. While he was overseas she worked with government agencies devising recipes for non-rationed foods and worked as food editor for Household Magazine.

In 1950 she returned to New York City; that year she and her husband were divorced. Vicki then joined Doubleday as a Literary Guild editor. In 1958 she married Armand Oppenheimer, an orthodontist who taught evolution of the teeth and mandibles at Columbia University and lectured at the Museum of Natural History. In his lectures and professional writing he stressed the environment as a controlling role in shaping the evolution of man and the primates. Fortunately for humankind, there were remarkable concurrences of major phenomena: the appearance of the angiosperms (flowering plants that bore fruit and seed and nectar), the evolution of the grasses and the discovery of the use of fire for cooking, tenderizing and making food a source of enjoyment.

Vicki became intensely interested in this field of study and enrolled as a graduate student at Columbia University. In 1963 she received a master's degree in Anthropology. She then pursued an exploration of food history in the New World and traveled to Mexico, Guatemala, Peru, Ecuador and Bolivia. She visited the sites where grasses, legumes, tubers and root crops were domesticated, cultivated and cross-bred to develop specimens suited to every environment and to a variety of tastes.

In 1991 she wrote "On the Nature of Food", now in its second edition. She continued her research on food, following a trail that led her to the Near East, Europe, Asia and Africa. The introduction of New World foods to Europe during the 16th and 17th centuries saved millions of people from starvation and enormously increased the entire world's food resources and tremendous population growth. "The Taste Makers" tells this dramatic story.

Vicki now lives in Naples, Florida. She is still vitally interested in world politics, education and, of course, food.

# The Artist

Mona Luisa Diogo was born in Luanda, Angola, in 1977. Her father was a Portuguese artist and her mother is an Angolan physician. She grew up in Angola and Portugal and came to the United States at the age of 15. She has studied art in Italy and Spain as well as in the United States, and she has exhibited her work in art galleries, museums and cafés in Boston, Massachusetts; Newport, Rhode Island; and Staten Island, New York. A Sociology graduate of Hunter College in New York City, she is currently working towards a graduate degree in Fine Arts, in Rome, Italy. When Mona is asked where she got her training, she replies "I have always drawn!"

# Index